"A true lover of Jesus, Marsha writes with pointed gentleness and compassionate straight talk that entices each of us to a better way of loving ourselves and trusting the God who made us for His glory. Whether you are a veteran of the faith or a new believer, whether you are facing formidable circumstances or have just come through the fire, as Marsha shares her own journey, you'll discover a yearning within for spiritual breakthrough and some practical helps to make it happen. Not only is the book a delight to read but it can be a powerful impetus toward change."

— TRICIA MCCARY RHODES, author of
Contemplating the Cross

"Marsha Crockett shows us in a powerful way how God works through the circumstances of our lives to draw us to Himself. I was moved by her courage to open up her heartaches so that I could relate and then to inspire me through the breakthroughs God had given her."

— NANCY DEMMITT, marriage and family counselor;
author of *Can You Hear Me Now?*

BREAK THROUGH

Unearthing God's Image to Find *the* Real You

Marsha Crockett

NAVPRESS®

OUR GUARANTEE TO YOU

For a free catalog
of NavPress books & Bible studies call
1-800-366-7788 (USA) or 1-800-839-4769 (Canada).

www.NavPress.com

The Navigators is an international Christian organization. Our mission is to advance the gospel of Jesus and His kingdom into the nations through spiritual generations of laborers living and discipling among the lost. We see a vital movement of the gospel, fueled by prevailing prayer, flowing freely through relational networks and out into the nations where workers for the kingdom are next door to everywhere.

NavPress is the publishing ministry of The Navigators. The mission of NavPress is to reach, disciple, and equip people to know Christ and make Him known by publishing life-related materials that are biblically rooted and culturally relevant. Our vision is to stimulate spiritual transformation through every product we publish.

© 2008 by Marsha Crockett

ISBN-13: 978-1-60006-185-1
ISBN-10: 1-60006-185-0

Cover design by studiogearbox.com
Cover image by Jae Rew/Photonica
Creative Team: Kris Wallen, Liz Heaney, Darla Hightower, Arvid Wallen, Kathy Guist

Some of the anecdotal illustrations in this book are true to life and are included with the permission of the persons involved. All other illustrations are composites of real situations, and any resemblance to people living or dead is coincidental.

Unless otherwise identified, all Scripture quotations in this publication are taken from the *HOLY BIBLE: NEW INTERNATIONAL VERSION*® (NIV®). Copyright © 1973, 1978, 1984 by International Bible Society. Used by permission of Zondervan Publishing House. All rights reserved. Other versions used include: *THE MESSAGE* (MSG). Copyright © 1993, 1994, 1995, 1996, 2000, 2001, 2002, 2005. Used by permission of NavPress Publishing Group; and the *English Standard Version* (ESV), copyright © 2001 by Crossway Bibles, a division of Good News Publishers. Used by permission. All rights reserved.

Published in association with the Books & Such Literary Agency, Janet Kobobel Grant, 52 Mission Circle, Suite 122, PMB 170, Santa Rosa, CA 95409-5370, www.booksandsuch.biz.

Library of Congress Cataloging-in-Publication Data

Crockett, Marsha, 1957-
  Break through : unearthing God's image to find the real you / Marsha Crockett.
     p. cm.
  Includes bibliographical references.
  ISBN-13: 978-1-60006-185-1
  ISBN-10: 1-60006-185-0
  1. Christian life. 2. Spiritual life--Christianity. 3. Spirituality. I. Title.
BV4501.3.C76 2007
248.4--dc22

                        2007032446

Printed in the United States of America

1 2 3 4 5 6 7 8 / 12 11 10 09 08

To Steve and Mary McQuinn,

whose lives bear witness to the wonder of how God's love breaks through in unexpected ways, at unexpected times, with unexpectedly divine results.

Contents

ACKNOWLEDGMENTS

At the end of a writing project I'm always stunned to find a clean manuscript stacked neatly on my desk. I usually can't recall how it happened, but I do remember notes and scribbles on odd pieces of paper, backs of envelopes, re-edited drafts, and miscellaneous notebooks. Eventually they all make their way to a typed form where they are again rearranged and shuffled around, scratched out, and written over. But somehow — through persistence, or wrestling over thoughts with God, or the fear of missing a deadline, or a little of all three — a finished manuscript appears.

This process, contrary to popular belief, is never a solitary one.

Without the work of my wonderful agent, Janet Kobobel Grant, I'd never make it out of the starting gate with my concepts.

Without the love and encouragement of faithful friends, especially my family — daughters, mother, brother, sister, aunts, uncles, cousins, nieces, nephews, and so many others who are physically no longer part of this world, I'd never make it past my self-doubts.

Without a team to critique, cajole, coach, and pray while I write — Joan Webb, Charlene Graham, and my sister, Linda Carlblom, in particular, as well as my long-standing writer's group,

Tuesday's Children, I'd never make it past my editor.

And without the good and gracious work of my editor, Liz Heaney, and the dedicated team players at NavPress, this book would never have found its way to the bookshelf and finally into the hands of a reader.

Above all, without God's ever-present Spirit of grace and truth, holding me, urging me, loving me, reaching me through this work, I'd never have reason to pick up my pen and write. I offer this book back to the Giver of words and life with an amazed yet grateful heart.

ONE

UNEARTHING GOD'S IMAGE IN US

Life often shifts, and that shift can cause friction, a rumbling, or even a cataclysmic upheaval in the way we live. It may leave us buried beneath the rubble of worry, fear, or confusion, frantic for the care and attention we desperately need from God. In such places we pray like the psalmist, "Turn your steps toward these everlasting ruins" (Psalm 74:3).

That's how I felt five or six years ago as I sat on the sofa, watching a television special with my daughter. It was one of those deeply inspiring, yet heart-wrenching reports of young children and their families who were surviving incredible odds in Africa in the midst of war-torn, crime-ridden neighborhoods. Though living in extreme poverty, the parents were dignified, honorable people. They were hopeful about the future, dreaming of a good education for their children. My daughter cried through most of the show, but not me. I sat like stone, unmoved, feeling distant and disconnected not only from the plight of these families but from my own emotions as well. Who or what had I become?

I had been aware of my lack of feeling more than once. The only emotion I seemed to experience was usually embarrassment over a seemingly "heartless" response. I even visited my doctor to rule out any medical problems. Physically all was normal. Yet inside, I had lost myself. I had an idea that brewing problems had something to do with my numbness. I assumed that by age forty-five or fifty I would have gotten over the who-am-I? phase of finding myself. I would never have thought that a few years later I would be writing a book about "discovering the real me." But then I hadn't expected a lot of things I was learning to cope with.

As I tried to adjust to the upheaval of suddenly being a single mother with a single income and a single car in need of repair, I sought to stay strong and unaffected by my raging emotions. But in time I sensed a hardening within me, and it didn't take long to see that the hardness carried a destructive force. My words were sharp, my attitudes judgmental, my moods dark, my tolerance nil, my relationships strained, and I didn't much like it.

Life had gotten tough, and I had tried to bury my problems and hide from the pain, but now the issues had become inflamed and life-threatening. Although the upheaval had not been my choice, I had added to the chaos by building emotional fences to hide the wreckage within. Things looked presentable from the outside . . . from a distance. But inside, close up, my desire to protect myself from additional pain had the potential to turn the core of my being into something hard and unrecognizable. That fear of being "frozen in mid-motion" — like the people of Pompeii or Lot's wife turned hard as a salt pillar — made me consider who I really wanted to be when I breathed my last breath.

NEW BEGINNINGS

I began to ask God to help me move on from this hard place in three ways:

First, I asked him to help me lose the pain of the past. It's easy to get stuck in old, hurtful thoughts, to sit and pick at a wound and never allow it to breathe and heal.

Second, I asked him to help me find my true identity as I journeyed forward. I wanted my life to express God's life in me. I wanted to speak with grace, to openly give and receive love.

And finally, I asked him to give me a renewed passion to live a meaningful life, to engage in deep relationships, and to enjoy the present moment, regardless of hardships the world set in my path.

I knew I had to decide how I wanted to live my life. If I chose to avoid the pain and the challenges, then I could continue in this tepid existence controlled by the barriers and obstacles in my path. Or, I could intentionally choose to change my thoughts, my actions, and my attitudes, and actually navigate through my life with the spiritual passion and freedom I claimed to possess as a follower of Christ. As you'll see, sometimes this meant facing new challenges and finding new dimensions of God's image within me. Other times it meant reclaiming that first love he had awakened in me years before and returning to that place of wonder.

In the days that followed my emotional disconnect, I began to search for God's hand and heart on this uphill climb out of the doldrums. I wanted to know what it meant to be created in his image. As I went back to the original Hebrew language, I learned that one meaning of *Imago Dei* is "shade." I smiled, thinking, *This puts a new twist to the idea of being "made in the shade!"* It reminded me of a day when I was walking through our neighborhood with my daughter when she was five or six years old. She skipped a few steps ahead of me, then came to a stop and pointed to the sidewalk and said, "Mommy, look how big my shadow is." I smiled, knowing that the shadow she saw was mine overshadowing hers.

As I remembered how my shadow had encompassed my daughter's, it became a vivid picture of how I experience God's image in me. The shadow of his presence is always with me — offering relief from the fires of life. As I considered God's inherent traits — his faithfulness, eternal presence, and point of view toward me — I learned to delight in who he is, and I began to unwrap his inexpressible gifts to equip me for the road ahead — gifts of hope, intimacy, peace, and freedom.

Ever so slowly I began to turn my life Godward. The prophet Isaiah set the direction for my journey. I kept these words close at hand, like checking the roadmap to make sure I was still on track.

Forget the former things; do not dwell on the past. See, I am doing a new thing! Now it springs up; do you not perceive it? I am making a way in the desert and streams in the wasteland . . . to give drink to my people, my chosen, the people I formed for myself that they may proclaim my praise. (Isaiah 43:18-21)

The prophet Ezekiel's words also brought special meaning to this journey and became my heart's desire, "I will give you a new heart and put a new spirit in you; I will remove from you your heart of stone and give you a heart of flesh" (36:26). Even now these words keep me pushing through toward real life when I feel buried beneath heartache, disappointment, anger, fear, or rejection. Over time I believe God has softened my heart, enriched my spirit, and allowed new life to break through the hard ground.

These sprouts of tenderness remind me of Jesus' story about a farmer who scattered seed on every imaginable type of soil on his property (see Matthew 13:1-23). I like to think of that soil as a map of my life at any one moment. Today my spirit may be hard and trampled down by too much foot traffic, as demands and responsibilities tread heavy on my time. Right next to the hard ground is a patch of untended earth, where weeds threaten to overtake an otherwise fertile plot. In some places I need to clear the land of rocks and boulders, to make straight paths. Or perhaps I need a miracle along the magnitude of water springing from a rock, such as God performed for Moses (see Exodus 17:1-6).

THE LAY OF THE LAND

Life is hard. How we handle those hard spots determines whether we become cynical or compassionate, angry or forgiving, imprisoned or free. If, when you look at the landscape of your inner being, it resembles a battleground, then I invite you to walk with me through these pages so we can survey the land together.

Each chapter that follows opens with words from Scripture and quotations from others whose wisdom speaks to the topic at hand. Use these words as a prayer-offering to prepare your heart and mind as you begin to excavate your inner being. I'll share my own journey to help you identify the hard places in life that threaten to leave you cold, unfeeling, or stuck in negative emotions. Then we'll begin to identify how God's image, his very presence and character, can begin to change us. At the close of each chapter you'll find practical and personal ways to break through in your life to discover how he equips you to move from old myths and lies into a place of grace and truth.

Use the journal suggestions and Scripture meditation exercises to further open your imagination and spirit, your body and mind to the Spirit of God as he speaks special words of comfort and counsel.

You may even want to find time for a personal *Break Through* retreat with God as you engage in these meditations.

I wish it were possible to take a picture of an individual and capture not only the physical image but also the spiritual, emotional, mental, and relational image as well. Then we could take "before" pictures of our lives as we begin this journey, and at the end of our time together, take "after" pictures. If it were possible, then I would show you my before image five or six years ago — an angry, hurt, and heartbroken woman stuck in defeated self-pity. Next to that image would be my after picture of the joyful, hopeful, growing, strong woman that I am becoming today.

Your life may feel like an uphill climb. But as you put one foot in front of the other, you will eventually reach a summit that breaks through to the breathtaking vistas that God has prepared just for you. He promises a new point of view, new horizons, and new paths to explore. In those moments when you discover God so close at hand, you'll see he is leading you to discover yourself in all the beauty of your God-given glory, and he is asking you to let him transform your heart of stone into a divine heart of flesh.

Two

Break Through to Blessing

Blessed are those whose strength is in you, who have set their hearts on pilgrimage . . . They go from strength to strength till each appears before God in Zion.

PSALM 84:5,7

Forget the former things; do not dwell on the past. See I am doing a new thing! Now it springs up; do you not perceive it? I am making a way in the desert and streams in the wasteland . . . to give drink to my people, my chosen, the people I formed for myself that they may proclaim my praise.

ISAIAH 43:18-21

All nature's wildness tells the same story: the shocks and outbursts of earthquakes, volcanoes, geysers, roaring, thundering waves and floods, the silent uprush of sap in plants, storms of every sort, each and all, are the orderly, beauty-making lovebeat of Nature's heart.

JOHN MUIR[1]

It was one of those days when I felt anger growling deep within —anger at my children for sneaking out windows into "forbidden territory" of late-night rendezvous with friends, anger at myself for getting stuck in distrust, unable to find the right gear to pull out of the rut, and anger at others for falling short of my expectations. I knew I sounded whiney at best, closer to victimized and bitter, embarrassingly bitter and blind to my own faults. It's nearly impossible for me to think my way out of anger, to logically douse the flames and prepare for new life to rise from ashes like the phoenix. Logic has no appeal in matters of the heart, and anger is as much a matter of the heart as is love.

So I scribbled a prayer into my journal: *Lord, keep me grounded in you, turned toward the cross, open to your truth, hungry for your touch, resting in your will, speaking through your grace. Lord, tender my life today.* If I couldn't keep myself from being consumed by negative emotions and the circumstances of life, then my only hope was in asking God to keep me . . . just keep me. These words struck me as odd and made me pay attention to what I was saying deep down. What did I mean? After all, our culture doesn't encourage women to be kept. Freedom flies in the face of being kept. Independence and self-determination laugh at the notion of giving yourself to another, and truly trusting that in this keeping you are safe.

My heart cry was much more than the casual, "Keep me posted." Or, "Keep me in mind," as if God is an absent-minded, overly-busy boss who needs a reminder to watch out for my interests. My request for God to *keep me* expressed something more. Too many times along the way I had felt emotionally beat up and left alone, like the wounded man who received the tender care of the Good Samaritan. My request was my 911 call to God to heal my wounds and bring me to a safe place where I could recuperate and regain my emotional and spiritual strength.

My cry spoke of my longing to be loved unconditionally and faithfully by one who speaks a language we mutually understand and knows my deepest needs even before I express them. My words unveiled my longing to be wanted and needed, longed for and pursued, treasured and not tossed aside. I was asking God to keep me as the apple of his eye, to keep me in perfect peace, to keep me ever before him, to keep me from falling, to keep me for all eternity. I was asking God to bless me.

A NEW NAME

Please understand. I wasn't asking God to do something for me; I wasn't asking him to "bless me" with a promotion or raise or new car or some other worldly gain. I cringe when I hear Christians slap the *blessing* label on such things. God's blessing isn't a label he slaps onto good fortune. Not that I'm ungrateful, but I refuse to believe that those with less physical abundance lack God's blessing. Such an attitude has the potential to turn God's goodness and blessing into a punitive tool to reward good behavior or punish the bad. The blessing is never in the gift or the increase. The blessing is in the relationship with the Giver.

So my request for God to bless me had more to do with his character and my identity than it did with my good fortune. Let me explain:

God's desire to bless us takes root in an ancient Jewish blessing, "The LORD bless you and keep you; the LORD make his face shine upon you and be gracious to you, the LORD turn his face toward you and give you peace" (Numbers 6:24-26). These words unearth God's tenderness toward us. He is the mother turning toward her baby, and we are the child who lights up, smiles, and reaches toward the face of love. God openly offers us this intimate face-to-face connection that results in mutual delight and peace, regardless of the surrounding challenges. This mother-child tenderness is further revealed in the Hebrew definition of the word *keep,* which alludes to a narrow view, with a focus solely on a particular point, and that point is you and I.

I am a bit undone by God's unabashed gaze, not because I'm afraid of what he might see in me, but because I'm unaccustomed to such attention. In a world competing for my time, my skill, and my money, with tactics of unceasing noise, mindless distractions, and a relentless pace, God's ever-present, quiet keeping makes me stop and consider his blessing. I don't possess the practiced grace of accepting this gift without a bit of skepticism. Yet God patiently pursues me. He treasures every moment of my life. My every breath is his to give. Along my journey he carries my burdens, relieves my worry, keeps attentive company every step of the way. This is what it means to walk with God.

Scripture tells us that Enoch "walked with God" (Genesis 5:22). Walking with another is also the meaning of the Greek word "comfort," which is used to describe the God of all comfort who walks alongside us (2 Corinthians 1:3). The "walking with God" attributed to Enoch derives from two Hebrew words implying crossroads and storytelling. Bound together they become a "tale-bearing journey." I love this thought that by allowing God to keep us "in the way we should go," he walks with us shoulder to shoulder, making our lives tale-bearing journeys of faith. God is there to comfort me and bless me even on those nights when I discover my teenager sneaking out a window, or when someone I love lies to me. He's there when I work through that hardness in my inner being that looks like the edge of a steep cliff and ties a knot in the pit of my stomach when I peer over the rim into the dark unknown.

Although the blessing of God's keeping comforts me, my habit of distrust provokes me to be suspicious of this spiritual wonder, and I can't stop myself from asking God why. Why would a grace-filled, glory-emanating God relentlessly pursue fear-driven, conflict-ridden humanity? It seems God anticipated our difficulty in accepting the *blessing of keeping*. He explained that when the blessing is given, it literally puts a new name on us (see Numbers 6:27). That name is God's name and is as infinite as his being. Listen to how he describes his name to Moses:

> *Then the* LORD *came down in the cloud and stood there . . . and proclaimed his name . . . "The* LORD, *The* LORD, *the compassionate and gracious God, slow to anger, abounding in love and faithfulness, maintaining love to thousands and forgiving wickedness, rebellion and sin." (Exodus 34:5-7)*

This is God's tender response to my disbelieving heart: *He has marked me as his own and given me his own name.* So, I claim this blessing on difficult days when anger growls deep within. I wrap his name — now my name! — around my ache. My name is *compassionate and gracious, slow to anger and abounding in love.* I sit with this blessing until I believe and become this name.

UNEARTHING GOD'S COMPASSION

Two things happen to me when I understand how God blesses me and keeps me and gives me his name. First, I grow in confident assurance that I belong to God as his own unique creation. Then, in that assurance I can view my own life — my attitudes, my words, and my actions — with compassion and grace, abounding in love. I'm not a perfect parent — I frequently throw pity parties, and I get frightened that I'm doing more harm than good to those I love. And yet, in God's compassion he blesses me and keeps me in order to complete me, and he meets my inadequacy with his adequacy when I cry out to him.

My heart cry may have been scribbled in my journal in a moment of desperation, but I have a sense that it has taken a lifetime for God to write it upon my heart. God's blessing is my identity. It is a force that courses through my life like a river through a canyon, etching itself deep into the bedrock of my resistance to love. How compassionate and so like God to use something as soothing as water to remove the rocky landscape of these difficult days. No hammer and chisels, no dynamite blasts — just a tender, constant flow, slowly changing the landscape of my world, marking me and making me recognizably his own. That flowing force drives out my anger, uproots my bitterness, and purifies my pain into passion. And I marvel that water gushes from a rock that is I.

BREAK THROUGH

1. Read the following verses that speak of God's power to keep you. Meditate on these truths. Choose one or two that speak most directly to your heart. What do these words mean for you? Tell God where you feel insecure and in need of his protecting attention. Now turn one of these verses into a prayer as you seek the blessing of keeping.

   ❧ "May the LORD keep watch between you and me." (Genesis 31:49)

   ❧ "You, O LORD, keep my lamp burning; my God turns my darkness into light." (Psalm 18:28)

   ❧ "Keep your servant also from willful sins; may they not rule over me." (Psalm 19:13)

⚜ "The LORD will keep you from all harm — he will watch over your life." (Psalm 121:7)

⚜ "You will keep in perfect peace him whose mind is steadfast." (Isaiah 26:3)

2. Find a quiet place and at least a few unrushed and uninterrupted minutes. Read Luke 10:25-37, the Parable of the Good Samaritan. Read it once aloud. Read it a second time silently and more slowly. Pause between verses and sentences and let God's Word wrap itself around you.

Now close your eyes and engage all your senses in the act of listening and receiving as you envision this story. Let your spirit listen to the Spirit of God. Put yourself in the place of the wounded man and put Christ in the place of the Good Samaritan. What do you see and hear? What do you sense through touch, smell, and taste? In this meditation notice how you have been wounded. How does Jesus' tender love speak to you, touch you, heal you, and bless you?

We don't know the rest of the man's story, but consider how the story might continue for you. In your journal, record your thoughts and experience of meditation and meeting Jesus in this way.

3. As you consider the name of God (see Exodus 34:5-7) as your blessing, what words draw your heart to his or touch your deepest need? Ask God to speak to you in a special way about this desire. Claim his name as your new identity in those places of need. Imagine what your heartaches look like in light of your new identity. Write what you see as a "before and after" description of your life.

4. Revisit the Scripture and quotation at the beginning of this chapter. Write a response to these words in your prayer journal.

THREE

BREAK THROUGH TO HOPE

Our bones are dried up and our hope is gone; we are cut off.

EZEKIEL 37:11

We who have run for our very lives to God have every reason to grab the promised hope with both hands and never let go . . . to be greatly encouraged. . . . We have this hope as an anchor for the soul, firm and secure . . . It's an unbreakable spiritual life-line . . . right to the very presence of God.

HEBREWS 6:18-20 (MSG AND NIV)

Spring seems far off, impossible, but it is coming. Already there is dusk instead of darkness at five in the afternoon; already hope is stirring at the edges of the day.

KATHLEEN NORRIS[1]

The phone rang. As soon as I heard my nineteen-year-old daughter say, "Mom . . ." I knew with a mother's instinct that something was wrong, deeply wrong. I had an inkling of an idea what it might be. In fact, it was a moment I dreaded and hoped for all at the same time.

"Megan, what is it?"

"I need help," she choked out the words between gulps and tears.

Only by God's Spirit of grace and peace did I not panic. Instead, I knew, with a child-of-God instinct, that all would be well. But I also knew it would be important for my daughter to articulate an important truth, so I calmly asked her, "What do you need help with?"

Silence. Then, "Drugs and lying."

These were the words I had waited, dreaded, and longed to hear my daughter say. In months past, we had talked, argued, yelled, and slammed doors over her out-of-control lifestyle. She had been through drug testing and counseling, with no life-changing result. Confronting an addict with truth can be as productive as tossing seed on cement, hoping it will yield a vegetable garden. But I knew that once an addict allows truth to rise up from within and embraces it, she is ready to enter recovery.

It wasn't until a few days later that hopelessness began to whisper in my ear. Megan had found an intensive outpatient rehabilitation program *on her own*, had made a payment to the counselor *on her own*, and had scheduled an appointment *on her own* for us both to discuss the program. But on the way to our meeting, she said, "What if it doesn't work? What if nothing can help? What if I can't do it?" It was as if she were reading my mind. This was the place and the point in time that I realized Megan would have to let go of control and shift her faith from her own abilities to God's ability. Would she be able to? So many addicts aren't able to sustain their recovery. Could Megan? I even wrestled with the possibility that my daughter could become another statistic, numbered among lives lost to drug and alcohol addiction. My questions buried hope and sent a chilling fear of failure through my bones.

Perhaps that's why I love Ezekiel's vision of dry bones and the dialogue between God and Ezekiel.

FROM DESPAIR TO HOPE

Ezekiel's prophecy of dry bones, spoken to the exiled people of Israel, gives us a dramatic picture of how God moves us from despair to hope. While it presents a graphic image of spiritual death, at the same time it unearths an almost whimsical delight in how God revives hope when it's needed the most.

Ezekiel describes the vision with these words: "I saw a great many bones on the floor," the lowest place of any dwelling. Then he emphasizes this lowest low point by saying, "on the floor of the valley" (37:2). When we're living on the floor in the lowest valley and around us is nothing but dry bones, when we've reached rock bottom, feel backed into a corner, up against a wall, our skeletal remains cry out, "Our bones are dried up and our hope is gone; we are cut off" (Ezekiel 37:11).

Cut off — that's how I felt — cut off from my natural instinct and dream for my child. That day when we drove to meet the counselor, I buried a simple dream that was birthed simultaneously with Megan's birth — that she would live a happy, productive life. I recognized my own rising despair in the realization that, indeed, her battle with addiction would require more inner strength and courage than I had ever seen her display thus far in her life.

At Ezekiel's ground zero, where his dreams for Israel lay scattered like corpses, the Spirit asks an interesting question, "Can these bones live?" (Ezekiel 37:3). I was asking this same question about my daughter: Can things ever change? Can this relationship be restored? Can this addiction be conquered?

Can these bones live?

At times everything we know about how to live is stripped away and we're left with the bare bones existence of making it from one step to the next. When there are no assurances of success or recovery or even life itself, we begin to ask tough questions. Yet it's only when we release our doubts and our control into God's hands that we can dare grasp onto hopefulness and respond in trust, as Ezekiel did, "O Sovereign LORD, you alone know" (37:3).

This honest response doesn't sing the praise of God's all-powerful, life-giving strength. Rather it is a prayer of worship and relinquishment that simply acknowledges that God is in control. His ways are beyond understanding, yet we put our life (and our possible death) into his hands and there rest in the contentment that claims, "It is well with my soul." Such an acknowledgment of God's sovereign faithfulness moves us from despair to hope.

As quickly as I faced the death of my dreams for my daughter, with equal haste God resurrected the gift of hope, and I began to believe again, in a new way, that whatever the obstacles, whatever the outcome, all would be well. In this hope I began to live. God's assurance and his faithfulness became the place where my thoughts would dwell.

HOPE TO ANCHOR THE SOUL

Tennyson wrote that it's "the mighty hopes that make us men."[2] Hope sets us apart from the animals. God-given hope is more than wishful thinking. Godly hope does not wish for something to happen. It confidently anticipates that an unbreakable promise is destined to occur. Hope is anchored in God's sovereignty. It's grounded in the truth that all things work for the good for those who love him (see Romans 8:28). It trusts in his unwavering love, in his immutable faithfulness.

Consider how God steadies us in the rough waters of life with these two hope-filled promises:

He claims us as his own. God's immediate response to our hopeless cry begins with the words, "O my people . . ." (Ezekiel 37:12). Without hope we are lifeless, lacking breath to whisper a prayer and muscle to move through an ordinary day. We lie in self-excavated graves of fear, waiting for life to return. Yet, in our hopelessness God claims us as his own.

These words literally help me feel God's arms around me, as if he is overcome with tenderness toward my despair and so gathers me close to his heart. It's the same response we hear from Jesus when he looks out over the valley of his people, and he cries out, "O Jerusalem, Jerusalem . . . how often I have longed to gather your children together, as a hen gathers her chicks under her wings" (Matthew 23:37). Such a claim sends the first shivers of life and hope through the marrow of the soul — the Redeemer, the Savior, not only rescues us from despair but, in fact, claims us as his own, as a promise to stay with us and to bring us to his second promise.

He gives us a place to dwell. God told Ezekiel, "I will put my Spirit in you and you will live, and I will settle you in your own land" (37:14). For the Israelites, this land was a literal geographic resting place they could call home. God has prepared a place for you and me to dwell as well — God himself is our dwelling place, settling us within the boundaries of his lovingkindness. King David knew this when he wrote, "You have been our dwelling place throughout all generations" (Psalm 90:1). And Paul confirmed that "In him we live and move and have our being" (Acts 17:28).

HOPE IN MOTION

The more I lived in the truth of God's sovereign faithfulness and reminded myself of it, the more the breath of life returned to me. It created a disturbance in the midst of my desperation that sent the dry bones rattling, and finally the breath of God entered those slain dreams. Hope makes us whole people, equips us to stay connected, standing and ready to move or dance or advance like an army. Now I was able to walk alongside my daughter, to encourage and offer her hope and assurance as she battled her addiction.

Moses had this kind of confident hope in God when he found himself and the Israelites wedged between an impassable sea on one side and a quickly advancing Egyptian army on the other. They had nowhere to turn except to God. And so they cried out to him. We know how the story ends — God parts the Red Sea. The Egyptian army is destroyed. The people rejoice. But we dare not skip over the explicit instructions Moses gave the people in the midst of a seemingly hopeless situation, for in these words we find the answer to the question that arises when we've encountered hope in our despair: Now what?

> Moses answered the people, "Do not be afraid. Stand firm and you will see the deliverance the LORD will bring you today. . . . The LORD will fight for you; you need only to be still." Then the LORD said to Moses, "Why are you crying out to me? Tell the Israelites to move on." (Exodus 14:13-15)

Three phrases stand out in this drama of last resorts. "Stand firm . . . be still . . . move on." We must also do these things in order to fully enter and receive the gift of hope.

Stand firm. When we lose our sense of hope, we lose just that, our ability to sense it. This doesn't mean hope has vanished, but rather that our eyesight is bad. Faith requires us to act on the truth of God's promises, regardless of what we see or fail to see. This is the key to standing firm, because when we're in an uncomfortable spot, our first reaction is to get out, to find our own form of comfort, to self-medicate, or reach for temporary distractions.

One week into my daughter's rehabilitation program, I came home from work long enough to pick her up and jump back in the car to drive her to her meeting. But when I walked in the house, I found her lying on the bathroom floor, drunk and sick. I had never seen her this way before. It was something she had previously hidden from me. Once again a sense of hopelessness rose from a dark place within me.

Did Megan have the strength to face this demon? I called the counselor's office. The person I spoke with reminded me that if my daughter was drunk she could not come to the group (a moot point since she couldn't even stand up, let alone walk into a group and participate). But their firm boundary and standard of recovery was enough to remind me to stand firm with her, even as God stood firm with me in his assurance that while this moment felt out of control, he was not. He was faithfully at work in my daughter's heart. Megan's return to her program the next day both confirmed her commitment and revealed her courage to stand firm on this journey.

Be still. This is perhaps the most difficult of the instructions, because when we feel panicked, hurt, or confused, we attempt to save ourselves from the steamroller bearing down on our lives. But stillness is what happens just before change occurs. When we are still, all movement ceases, and we stop to experience a change of direction. Stillness speaks in the moments before a tornado tears through the land, or before a butterfly emerges from the cocoon.

Stillness does not mean we do nothing. It means simply relaxing in God-confident behavior to still the fear, to quiet the incessant hum of control, and to trust that God sees, knows, cares, and is at work. Rarely does God tell his people to stop crying out to him. But there is a time to stop fussing — maybe even to stop praying for the same thing over and over — and to move to the next step.

Move on. I've known Christians who never seem to move past old wounds, failures, or losses, who repeatedly cry out for forgiveness for the same mistakes. In fact, I've been that Christian. But I'm tired of living that way. I am beginning to believe it's time to be still, to stop crying out, and to start begging for eyes to see God's faithfulness to me, despite my doubts. This gift greatly encourages me to lift my head, to focus on what lies before me.

But when we get stuck in an emotion (or in the attention we receive from emotional drama), we fail to realize that we're free to move on. The "fasten seat belt" light is off, and it's time to unfasten what holds us back, to stand up, and move on. "Throw off everything that hinders and entangles and run the race" (Hebrews 12:1, paraphrased). This is especially difficult when the entanglement gives us temporary satisfaction and pleasure, such as the euphoria of a chemical high. But during times like these, hope does its deepest work. Without a hope that rises above the fleeting, feel-good pleasures, we find little reason to change.

This was true for me, and it was also true for Megan. She hoped she could live life with authentic emotions rather than a foggy, drug-induced numbness and enjoy real relationships rather than using people as a means to her addictive behavior. As for me, my hope that God's plan for my daughter was better than even my biggest dreams for her enabled me to release the temporary satisfaction of trying to control and save her. Megan had her own journey to walk. Sure our paths ran close together, but I needed to get out of her lane and give her room to navigate that road.

UNEARTHING GOD'S SOVEREIGN FAITHFULNESS

I can't say that I'm a pro at any of this. It takes courage to stand firm when I feel as if I'm melting inside. It takes discipline to be still before God when I'm crying in fear. And it takes strength to engage the gears to move onward when I'm uncertain where we're headed. But I remember God's faithfulness, that he champions not just a cause but he champions his people, "O my people . . ."

After Megan cried out for help, she found her own promised land with the professionals and recovering addicts alike who walked with her through eighteen weeks of intensive recovery. She joined an Alcoholics Anonymous group and began the hard work of the 12-step program. Now, over two years later, Megan remains clean. She shows me nearly every day how to stand firm in a commitment, how to be still enough to let go of controlling those things she cannot change, and how to find the courage to move on.

When my dreams for my daughter turned to dry bones, God breathed new hope into my life as well — a hope grounded in the assurance that whatever the circumstances, all will be well, for hope is that unbreakable lifeline holding us firm and secure, leading us into the very presence of God.

BREAK THROUGH

1. When or where have you felt hopeless? In what areas of your life do you feel stuck, as if things will never change? Can you identify the dreams that you have let die? How have these "hopeless" spots threatened to become barren, neglected, or lifeless ground in your life? Record these recollections in your journal. Offer them to God. Without any preconceived notions of what God may do in these situations, visualize your writing as a valley of dry bones. Ask God to breathe life where it is needed, to restore hope where there is none, to reconnect pieces scattered across the landscape of your

soul. Over the next week, be mindful of how your heart, your prayers, your thoughts, your actions may change ever so slightly. Examine and reflect on these movements of change at the end of each day. Record your discoveries in your journal.

2. Read the following verses:
    *   "May those who fear [honor] you rejoice when they see me, for I have put my hope in your word." (Psalm 119:74)
    *   "The LORD delights in those who fear him, who put their hope in his unfailing love." (Psalm 147:11)
    *   "Hope deferred makes the heart sick, but a longing fulfilled is a tree of life." (Proverbs 13:12)
    *   "Christ in you, the hope of glory." (Colossians 1:27)
        Identify the solid ground where Scripture encourages us to find hope. How have you experienced this hope? In what ways do you long to experience this hope? How might such hope stabilize your life? What role does hope play in your relationships (friendships, family, faith community)?

3. Consider the three instructions to the Israelites at the Red Sea: Stand firm. Be still. Move on. What do these words mean to you in the challenges and low spots you face right now. Which do you most need to hear and act upon? What are those things that entangle you or hinder you from "running the race" in your spiritual journey?

4. Revisit the Scriptures and quotation at the beginning of this chapter. Write a prayer in response to these words.

Four

Break Through to Peace

Dying to self is not about what you give up but what you gain.

Tricia McCary Rhodes[1]

The punishment that brought us peace was upon him, and by his wounds we are healed.

Isaiah 53:5

Hast thou no scar?
No hidden scar on foot or side or hands?
I hear thee sung as mighty in the land.
I hear them hail thy bright ascendant star,
Hast thou no scar?

Hast thou no wound?
Yet I was wounded by the archers, spent
Leaned Me against a tree to die: and rent
By ravening beasts that encompassed Me, I swooned
Hast thou no wound?

No wound? No scar?

Yet as the Master shall the servant be,

And pierced are the feet that follow Me;

But thine are whole: can he have followed far

Who has no wound nor scar?

AMY CARMICHAEL[2]

I was young when I first read the words of Amy Carmichael's "Hast Thou No Scar?" It was one of the first times I felt prompted to take a "spiritual inventory" of my life, trying to determine if I, like Jesus, had a scar. While I had a rocky adolescence (who didn't?), and was dumped by or had dumped several boyfriends, I really couldn't find any scars. Did that mean I lacked a sincere faith? And then there was that Bible verse I kept remembering where Jesus says, "Take up [your] cross and follow me" (Matthew 16:24). I was certain that if I really wanted to prove my love for Jesus, I should be looking for some terrible way to live for him.

But over the years it's become clear to me that we don't have to go looking for crosses to bear. We live with burdens, heartaches, disappointments, poor choices, sadness, and loneliness. Our crosses seem to define our human experience and threaten to keep our lives in turmoil. It doesn't take long, living in this world, to realize that pain and loss are the inevitable part of living.

As I pushed my food around the plate with my fork, wondering if my appetite would ever return, I knew this to be true. I was in the middle of a life-upheaval, unsure if I had the strength or courage to rebuild my reality even though I knew it had to be done. My eighteen-year marriage had come to a screeching halt. Now the wheels were in motion to finalize the divorce. I had to find work substantial enough to make ends meet for my daughters and me and an affordable home for us to live in. I also needed a faith strong enough to regain my confidence and move forward into whatever God had planned beyond this heartbreaking moment.

In such cross-bearing seasons the challenge isn't necessarily to bear the cross. The challenge is to *follow Jesus* on the path toward peace rather than follow the pain or the loss on a path toward bitterness or resentment. We lose our direction in following Jesus because we think his promise of peace means protection from suffering. We miss the truth he laid out in the Upper Room conversation with his disciples when he spoke of experiencing peace *and* suffering, joy *and* mourning. "I have told you these things so that in me you may have peace. In this world you will have trouble. But take heart! I have overcome the world" (John 16:33).

SECOND TAKE

We can't escape our weeping and mourning, grieving and pain. But in the midst of our heartache, God has given us a gift for our healing and wholeness. He has appointed blessing in the midst of burdens, if we have the courage to embrace it by first letting go of these oft-repeated myths about our suffering that keep peace from entering in.

Myth #1 — We suffer because of sin in our lives. When they came upon a man who had been crippled from birth, the disciples asked Jesus, "Whose fault is it that he's crippled? Who sinned, him or his parents?"

Jesus responded, "Neither." Then, revealing a more compassionate way to look at suffering in the context of who God is, he explained, "You're asking the wrong question. . . . You're looking for someone to blame. There is no such cause-effect here. Look instead for what God can do. This happened that the work of God might be displayed in his life" (John 9:3, paraphrased).

God isn't a get-even God, a do-something-wrong-and-I'll-get-you God. Of course the choices we make, good or bad, have natural consequences, but God wants to restore our lives, to redeem our mistakes, and to relieve our burdens, not make them heavier. To believe otherwise is to render Christ's sacrifice pointless.

The truth is, it makes no difference why we suffer, whether from sin or circumstance or acts of nature. Suffering is unavoidable in this world. For this reason God promises that he will make our suffering matter by giving it purpose and the potential to reveal his heart of compassion and comfort and mercy, thus bringing us to a place of peace. "Rejoice that you participate in the sufferings of Christ, so that you may be overjoyed when his glory is revealed" (1 Peter 4:13).

Myth #2 — If my faith were strong, I wouldn't have to bear this cross. This is simply not true. After all, whose faith was stronger than Job's? God allowed Job's suffering because of his strong faith, not his weak faith. And it is said, even of Jesus, that "Although he was a son, he learned obedience from what he suffered" (Hebrews 5:8). The cross we bear is an invitation for our faith to flourish.

Yet people sometimes think that the reason God hasn't answered their prayer is that their faith is weak, and so they continue to live in turmoil over the cross they bear. Personally, I don't believe in *unanswered* prayer. I wish all Christians would eliminate this phrase and belief from their minds. God hears and responds to *all* prayer, whether we get our *wish* or not.

God hears every prayer offered, spoken or unspoken, and he responds to it. Sometimes we are aware of his response; sometimes we aren't. Still, prayer always affects us and it always affects God. He is working far beyond our realm of imagining and far beyond our desire for personal comfort and easy living. To say God didn't answer my prayer is to believe that God is ignoring me or doesn't care. I believe that just as some animals can hear sound beyond the human audio frequency, so too God hears our prayers and responds to them at frequencies higher than our human capacity to comprehend.

Myth #3 — It's not God's will to "take this cup" from me. Nonsense. It is completely *within* God's will for his creation to be whole and redeemed and to be at peace with themselves, their world, and with God. Sin and suffering were not part of God's original plan. Yet we believe this myth because we are pain-avoiders and comfort-seekers. Our vision of an easy life is myopic, our plans self-centered, our desire for comfort nearly idolatrous. So we get angry and defensive when we encounter trouble or loss and accuse God of being heartless by allowing us to suffer. How could a loving God permit his children to suffer in such profound ways in this world? God does not delight in seeing his children suffer any more than we delight in seeing our own children suffer. "In all their distress he too was distressed" (Isaiah 63:9).

Yet suffering and loss remain in this age as a result of our separation in paradise. Only through Christ are we restored and our losses redeemed. Redemption is the act of taking something of seemingly little value and exchanging it for something of greater value or worth. And while we would never claim that Christ's life was of "little value," the fact is it was only one life that God exchanged for the salvation of all humanity.

The physical and emotional effects of sin continue to touch our lives, yet the consequences of sin and suffering have lost the power to destroy us spiritually. So while God allows the course of nature to rule this world for now, he has taken spiritual death out of the equation. He is willing to transform our pain and give us peace, if we are willing to follow his lead.

THE SIGNPOSTS OF PEACE

Bear in mind that our experience of taking up the cross differs from Jesus' experience in that our pain and loss and heartaches are not always something we plan for or expect. Jesus knew what was ahead for him. The road that led to Golgotha was no surprise. For us, dreams and relationships often come crashing to an unexpected end. We've had no time to process the journey, but suddenly we're at the end of the road. We don't have the long night of the passion to struggle with our own will. We're caught off guard by loss and death and pain and problems. We sit dazed, pushing our food around on a plate, forgetting what to do next.

Yet despite these differences, if we follow the example Jesus set as he took up his cross, we can begin to break through our pain to experience peace through God's abiding comfort.

Vigilance. The night before Jesus was about to take up his cross, he asked Peter, James, and John to come to the Garden of Gethsemane and to "watch and pray" with him (Mark 14:34,37,38). Nothing eases the burden of our cross more quickly than a faithful friend who is willing to watch and pray with us. As we bear the burdens together, we vigilantly watch for God at work in the midst of the pain. We pray for eyes to see his presence and peace and we invoke his name and his blessing on one another. The vigil of friendship and the call to watch and pray isn't a call to smile and offer easy answers or a call to try to fix the problem or pretend it didn't happen at all.

My friend Karen understands this. When I went through those first difficult days of transition following my divorce, she sat across from me at countless lunch meetings. She often pushed her food around her plate with me. She gave no pat answers, and I recall only a few words of comfort. But what I remember most is a simple awareness that in her presence I felt God's nearness, and my fears subsided when she stood on watch with me.

When loss first knocks on our door, we don't open it and immediately understand why we have to experience the heartache. When my marriage ended, the emotional trauma felt pointless. But the experience has transformed me because I allowed God to transform my heart through his healing. It took months to get beyond sad. It took years to get back on my feet. But the gift of those faithful ones who watched and prayed with me has never left me. Their prayers saw me through and unearthed God's desire to walk with me through the pain. It allowed me to experience first-hand the promise that nothing can separate me from the love of God (see Romans 8:38-39). I may not always get the point of my pain or loss. I may never realize a greater good. But I believe, without exception, that God infuses my suffering with meaning and purpose for the greater glory of his kingdom. And this is all I need to know.

Grace. When Peter used his weapon to cut off a soldier's ear, Jesus said, "Put down your sword," and in the place of wounding he brought healing. Then when Jesus' accusers mounted false charges against him, he again refused to take a defensive posture. His silence was another means of putting down the sword. How difficult this must have been, given his attackers and mistreatment. But didn't Jesus' silence disturb his accusers more than a slick and wordy defense? Grace disarms. For if no defense is offered, no offense can be returned.

I discovered the wisdom of this when I determined shortly after my marriage ended that for the sake of my daughters I would speak no accusation against their father. Neither would I publicly belittle him or discuss the issues leading to the divorce. Certainly I processed my emotions and my pain with my closest friends and a counselor, but never to be shared in a destructive or degrading way. No, this was not an easy choice, but it was an intentional choice, one I frequently had to renew within myself. To those who knew me and my family, to my faith community, the silence spoke far beyond the issue of divorce. It spoke to my desire to forgive and move forward. For this I am forever grateful that God would choose to use my cross to strengthen me as well as many others in the body of Christ.

Forgiveness. When I come to the words of Christ forgiving his executioners, and forgiving all humanity, I see more than an example of how I should forgive others who have hurt me. I hear Jesus' words directed to me. I too don't know what I do. I don't know how my actions have crucified the embodiment of God. I don't know the true cost of Jesus' sacrifice, so following Jesus first means asking for forgiveness. *Father, forgive me, for I don't know what I do. I gloss over sin, I ignore opportunity, I speak when I should be silent, and I'm silent when I should speak.*

Following Jesus while carrying my cross also means I need to offer forgiveness to those who have hurt me. Jesus said: "If you do not forgive men their sins, your Father will not forgive your sins" (Matthew 6:15). When I refuse to offer forgiveness to others, it hardens my heart to the point that I stop asking forgiveness or even seeing the sin in my own life, and I miss the promise to experience "peace like a river" (Isaiah 48:18). My own hardness of heart can prevent me from *receiving* God's forgiveness, not because God isn't willing to forgive me but because I am blind to my own sin.

I was reminded of this recently during an early Friday morning small-group gathering when a friend shared a struggle she faced in her workplace. She had been blamed and verbally berated by her boss for something in which she had no culpability. My friend is as close to God as anyone I know, and her spirit as authentically tender and encouraging as I've ever witnessed. I felt indignant over the incident, but she remained calm and simply said, "All I know is that as a Christian woman I'm called to forgive and love and never hold a grudge. Maybe it will make a difference somehow, in him or in me. Who knows?"

I felt like one of Job's friends who had offered all the wrong answers and given unwise advice. I was amazed, as I often am, by her Christ-centered response. To lighten the mood, I responded, "All I know is that as a *bitter* Christian woman, I don't think I could respond like that." We all laughed and agreed it was much easier to be bitter about being wronged.

On my way to work later that morning, I thought more quietly about the *bitter* part of my reaction. It may have been a joke, but it was too easy to allow that feeling to rule over my life. I'm quick to judge others, quick to want to hit back when someone strikes at me or my friends. I prayed and wondered, *When will I ever grow out of that? And why should I be so bitter, Lord?*

That's when Jesus reminded me that he drank the bitter cup for me on his way to the cross, so I wouldn't have to be bound by bitterness in moments like this. He drained it completely and swallowed every drop, allowing me to enter instead into the creative ministry of reconciliation. This remembrance allowed me to release my resentment and break through to Christ's peace, freeing me to pray life and blessing into my friend's situation and even into the life of her boss.

The difficulty of forgiving others comes when I believe I have acted righteously and that the injustice and suffering has come from the hand of another. Yet I have no claim to self-righteousness. I am as much a part of the brokenness in this world as anyone who inflicts pain upon me. Until I can let go of my own righteousness, I cannot abandon myself to God's righteousness. Until I acknowledge my own responsibility in the mess of humanity, I cannot claim the grace that softens my hard-heartedness with peace.

Only in the ancient and honored prayer of the ages, "Lord, have mercy," am I prepared to receive healing. Only when I intentionally choose to put down the defense of anger and resentment and rest in the trustworthy hands of God does he begin to instill a quiet harmony in me. *Father, forgive me even as I learn to forgive myself.*

Devotion. In his ability to forgive the world, Jesus revealed his divinity; in his proclamation, "I thirst," he revealed his humanity. Our suffering and loss often leave us hungering and thirsting for God in deeper ways. I remember in the weeks after my dad died, my mother said she just couldn't get enough of God's Word. She clung to it and drank deeply from the river of peace that only the Spirit can offer. Rather than complaining about our thirst as we bear our crosses, or quenching it with temporary worldly pleasures, perhaps we should be praying, *Lord, let me thirst for you more.*

The paradox in thirsting for God is that while he quenches our thirst, he also instills it. Thomas Pierson put it this way, "If we have a godly thirst, it will appear by diligence in frequenting the place and means of grace; brute beasts for want of water will break through hedges, and grace thirsty souls will make their way through all encumbrances to come where they may have satisfaction."[3] The purpose of this passionate thirst is to bring our hearts to a place of worship and ever-deepening devotion.

UNEARTHING GOD'S PEACE OFFERING

I explored what it means to experience peace in the midst of suffering at the opening of the Advent season. It felt odd because it seemed more appropriate to be turned toward Bethlehem and the manger rather than toward Jerusalem and the cross. That's when I stumbled upon this realization: At Christ's birth, the angel-filled heavens sang, "Glory to God in the highest, and on earth peace to men" (Luke 2:14). Thirty-three years later, when Jesus entered Jerusalem, heading toward the cross, the people sang out to the heavens, "Peace in heaven and glory in the highest!" (Luke 19:38).

In this antiphonal refrain heaven sings, "Peace on earth." And the earth responds, "Peace in heaven." The low, harmonious chant of these two melodies — "Son of God . . . Son of Man" — forms a bridge. At this juncture where the cross is driven deep into the earth and stretches high toward the heavens, peace reigns between the open arms of Christ. Only the divine humanity of Jesus can rejoin what sin has put asunder. His death — the bloody suffering and battered dying of the innocent Lamb of God — culminates in a messy colliding of holiness and humanity.

When I gaze upon that scene it's hard to discern where Jesus' humanity and divinity start and stop. The tension between the two is seen every step of the way in the journey to the cross. But the fact that Jesus struggled gives me hope and an awareness that in my life, messy as it is, struggle as I may, wrestle as I do with being a child of God, yet he lives in me and reveals himself to me. When I'm willing to join my heart to his, I begin to understand that when life feels heavy and I'm tempted to follow my pain rather than follow Jesus, even then he is working to bring forth peace through his passionate suffering and loving sacrifice. We will have trouble in this world. But take heart. The way of the cross paves the path to peace, and by his wounds, we are healed.

BREAK THROUGH

1. What beliefs have you had about your own suffering and losses? How have they affected you in a positive or negative way? What is your response to the myths about suffering identified in this chapter?

2. Draw out a timeline of your life and label your cross-bearing seasons or dates on one side of the line. Now on the opposite

side of that line, label how God may have used those times to develop you or change you or to reveal himself to you. Do you see a pattern in your life or a consistent purpose for these challenges?

3. What did Jesus say or do on his journey to the cross that you need to practice in your own journey? To watch and pray, to forgive, to thirst? What else might you add? How have these signposts led you to a place of peace?

4. Read and meditate on one of the following verses: Colossians 2:13-15; Philippians 2:5-11; Philippians 3:7-11. Sit with these words over several days. Memorize those verses or phrases that God is impressing on you. How do these words about suffering and the cross reveal life and power in you today? What does God ask of you as you hold these words in your heart?

5. Revisit the Scriptures and quotes at the beginning of this chapter. Write a prayer in response to these words.

FIVE

BREAK THROUGH TO FREEDOM

You desire truth in the inner parts; you teach me wisdom in the inmost place.

PSALM 51:6

Our souls were created in the image and likeness of God. . . . How unfortunate that we do not really understand ourselves . . . because we so seldom consider the nature and quality of our inner life. . . . And so we make little effort to guard or nurture the soul's beauty . . . we focus on the outer walls of the castle, while within the treasures of heaven lie in waste.

TERESA OF AVILA[1]

To say that the desert has no water is a tantalizing mistatement. It is believable. But to look over this raven land and know the truth — that there is immeasurable water tucked and hidden and cared for by bowls of rock, by sudden storms . . . is by far a greater pleasure and mystery than to think of it as dry and senseless as wadded newspaper.

CRAIG CHILDS[2]

Not long ago I attended a business event where a life coach asked us to participate in an exercise where we introduced ourselves to one another. We were required to come up with three adjectives and a noun that would describe who we are. It had to be positive and the noun could not be a role that we play. One couldn't say "I am a dedicated, focused, fair boss." We had to define ourselves by something other than a role.

I smiled at how quickly I was able to complete the exercise, remembering how intimidated and anxious I would have felt a few years earlier when I was struggling to find my own identity beyond what I did for others. Now I was having so much fun with this exercise, I wrote out several options and had trouble choosing which words suited me best: "Beautiful, intelligent, independent woman" or "A unique, inspiring, generous individual," or some other combination of words (perhaps including humble?).

The woman next to me stared at her paper for several minutes, took a deep breath, exhaled loudly in frustration, and finally raised her hand to ask, "What if I'm not yet any of the positive words that I want to be?" I admired her for voicing such a vulnerable question. One of her adjectives should have been *truthful*.

The life coach gently responded, "If you have the desire to be those words, that desire came from somewhere within you. So the essence of those traits is already true of you. Maybe you're just finding better ways to let those truths express themselves in your life." I liked that thought and was glad she said it. Even though I was able to find my own positive truth rather quickly (at least on this day), it eased my mind when it came time to introduce myself. "My name is Marsha, and I'm a creative, fearless, contented child of God."

Some would argue that being a child of God is a role, but to me it is the essence of who I am. It is my birthright, given to me before the dawn of time, and it will be mine throughout eternity. This exercise helped me see what a journey it has been to come to a place where I am open to the truth of my life, and it looks beautiful to me. In the past I've been skeptical about such exercises and quick to label them as self-centered, pop psychology. I've dismissed them with a wave of superiority as shallow, feel-good, mind games. But when backed by the immutable strength and character of a loving God, such an exercise has the power to transform our lives and build up our faith on a solid foundation of truth. So these days I'm asking God to help me grow up to be his child so that I can retrace the steps that lead to the truth of who I am because of him.

God is always calling us to see truth at the core of our inner being. He calls us to know ourselves as he knows us — to acknowledge the truth about ourselves. Although not fully defined in Scripture, the inner being is referred to numerous times.

- "Surely you desire truth in the *inner parts*; you teach me wisdom in the inmost place." (Psalm 51:6)
- "Your beauty . . . should be that of your *inner self*, the unfading beauty of a gentle and quiet spirit, which is of great worth in God's eyes." (1 Peter 3:3-4)
- "I pray that out of his glorious riches he may strengthen you with power through his Spirit in your *inner being*." (Ephesians 3:16)

I like to think of the inmost place as the studio of the soul, the place where God speaks and lives in me and is busy crafting me into his vessel. It's where my character sits atop the potter's wheel, and where the Spirit of Truth, the Counselor, sculpts out truth and casts off lies to unveil the real me. Knowing and desiring inner truth is nearly impossible without the interceding work of the Spirit. The Spirit doesn't just express God's point of view in God's voice. Part of the Spirit's mystery and ministry is to communicate our inner being to God as well. The Spirit not only speaks God's truth, but he also expresses our reality to God. He translates the human experience into divine dialogue "with groans that words cannot express" (Romans 8:26).

When we are open to God's truth in our inner life, we find a comfortable sense of freedom to be ourselves. But when we deny that truth, we often feel trapped in a farce that can wreak havoc on the soul.

IDENTITY THEFT

When I was in my early twenties I remember feeling like I was stuck on a church pew looking out at the world, and it looked like those in the world were having all the fun. So with only slight encouragement from some coworkers, I decided to try to live as "free" as the law permitted. I ignored my God-given boundaries. In the name of "fun" I drank too much, stayed out too late, ran with a rough crowd, and hated every minute of it. This lifestyle simply was not true to who God created me to be. I've always been more introspective and quiet. Trying to be otherwise felt miserable and seemed an act of disloyalty to myself if not to God.

If I allow the opinions of others to shape my understanding of who I am, then I'm giving them authority over my identity and denying the power of God to shape my heart, mind, and spirit. If I try to be someone other than who I am, then I'm telling God that his design is flawed, and I close the door to living at peace with him and with myself.

That's exactly what Adam and Eve did. I often think about that moment when they sinned. It's easy to believe they sinned by eating the fruit that God forbade. But if this were the case — that their sin was only about the tree, the fruit, and the eating — then God is not much more than a legalistic control freak.

The longer I dwell on this passage, the more I believe that the original sin, and all subsequent sin, occurs when we allow lies and deception to steal our identity by tempting us away from being who God created us to be. At that point, along with Adam and Eve, we enter an illusion that we lack something, which causes us to want something different from what God created us to be.

So we choose to carry a fake identity, cut from the fabric of a lie, and deny our true beauty. We hide ourselves from God, hoping he won't see how we have destroyed his intention toward us. In essence we label the beauty of our existence as inferior workmanship. Sin, then, is not so much about breaking a law as it is breaking the heart of God by diminishing his love for us and in us.

Lies fragment our lives by wedging themselves between heart and soul, mind and body. This sends schisms through our lives that separate the physical from the emotional and the spiritual from the intellectual, which can affect our self-perception by blurring our God-awareness. We experience this when we're afraid to use our logical minds in the spiritual realm; perhaps we fear our questions and reasoning will tear apart our faith. If that is a possibility, then maybe our so-called faith needs to be dismantled so that God can rearrange our thinking and strengthen the structure of our beliefs. Or, perhaps our emotion seems dislocated from our belief systems, such as when I expend energy worrying until it affects my physical well-being.

But we don't have to live this way. God has called us to live a better way. He has invited us to live in the freedom of truth.

CALLED TO LIVE IN TRUTH

Webster defines *truth* as "revealed or not concealed." The Spirit works to bring us and keep us in a state of being unconcealed. Paul speaks of this in 2 Corinthians 3:16-18:

> *Whenever anyone turns to the Lord, the veil is taken away. Now the Lord is the Spirit, and where the Spirit of the Lord is, there is freedom. And we, who with unveiled faces all reflect the Lord's glory, are being transformed into his likeness with ever-increasing glory.*

As we place our lives more fully in Christ's keeping, we will gradually and naturally see the truth about our identity. This truth sets us free.

Let me give you an example of what this looks like. A few years ago a friend told me she had kept a secret locked up inside her. She feared it was going to eat her alive, and her relationships along with it, if she didn't confess it. So, with trembling hands and tear-filled eyes she told me the story of how fifteen years earlier she had aborted her baby. I'm no counselor. All I knew was to listen, love, and accept my friend in light of the God-given grace I'd experienced in my own life.

Once she was open to facing the truth, God began to reveal more of it to my friend, and things began to open up in new ways for her. The truth that shattered her false identity was Jesus' unconditional grace toward her. He showed her that her true identity was not wrapped up in her heartache, failure, or sin. She experienced the truth that her baby is a beloved child, safe in the arms of God, and that all things, placed in the loving hands of God, work together for good. My friend's healing is an ongoing journey that has touched the lives of women with whom she has shared her story. Her truth gives others courage to unveil their own story and to receive truth and grace and live in freedom.

Consider these additional reasons why God calls us to be truth-loving people:

Truth is the touchstone of Jesus' life. It marks his words. Countless times in the gospels, Jesus punctuates his teaching with the words, "I tell you the truth." Truth permeates his message. He "came from the Father, full of grace and truth" (John 1:14). He personifies truth. "I am . . . the truth" (John 14:6). As I work through my own identity, I believe the Spirit asks me to claim this phrase *I am the truth* as a standard for measuring my authenticity. Not that I am the ultimate saving truth for all humanity, but rather *I am living the truth* by living as God created me to be.

These words have become a yardstick for truth in my life, especially when I struggle with the cognitive dissidence that clues me in to inner conflict between what I believe and how I behave. For instance, Jesus tells me in no uncertain terms, "Do not worry about your life" (Matthew 6:25). Yet, I expend enormous amounts of time worrying about things that never come to pass. This is when I ask myself, "Am I living the truth that I need not worry? Can I claim that I am that truth?" If the way I'm living doesn't display God's truth, then I have some work to do, and the Spirit has work to do within me.

Truth refreshes the heart and pleases God. It's easy to miss this. We sometimes think that if we know the truth about ourselves, the only things we'll see are failure, mistakes, disappointment, incompetence, and a dozen other ways in which we've fallen short. This is why truth must be accompanied by the Spirit of God. This is why Jesus came full of truth *and* grace. For every weakness we uncover in our search for truth, God appoints a greater strength to replace it. Paul knew this about his identity in Christ, "For when I am weak, then I am strong" (2 Corinthians 12:10).

Be assured that the voices of shame and self-condemnation that speak in our minds with such harshness are not of God. These voices are the illusions others have spoken into us. When we accept what they say as the complete truth about ourselves, they keep us far from God. But when we begin to turn away from these lies and turn instead toward God (this is the definition of repentance), then a miracle occurs. We are no longer enslaved to the lies but rather have entered a time to be refreshed. "Repent, then, and turn to God, so that your sins may be wiped out, that times of refreshing may come from the Lord" (Acts 3:19). That's exactly how I felt when I set aside the "party girl" phase of my life. I felt as if I had come back home to myself, and I breathed a sigh of relief.

UNEARTHING GOD'S LIBERATING TRUTH

So how do we recognize and reclaim ourselves and live in the freedom of being true? God has explicitly written our identity throughout Scripture. He leaves no question about who we are in his view. Here are a few of my favorite truths about my identity that I've gleaned from God's Word. I was tempted to expound on what each of these means to me, but I've chosen to allow God to speak directly into your heart his own words without my running interference. Read through these truths once, then go back and read them again more slowly, letting them steep in your heart and mind:

- *I am God's workmanship.* "For we are God's workmanship, created in Christ Jesus to do good works, which God prepared in advance for us to do." (Ephesians 2:10)
- *I am chosen.* "But you are a chosen people . . . a people belonging to God, that you may declare the praises of him

who called you out of darkness into his wonderful light."
(I Peter 2:9)

❧ *I am a letter from Christ.* "You show that you are a letter from Christ, . . . written not with ink but with the Spirit of the living God, not on tablets of stone but on tablets of human hearts." (2 Corinthians 3:3)

❧ *I am a living stone.* "You also, like living stones, are being built into a spiritual house to be a holy priesthood, offering spiritual sacrifices acceptable to God through Jesus Christ." (I Peter 2:5)

❧ *I am the light of the world.* "For God, who said, 'Let light shine out of darkness,' made his light shine in our hearts to give us the light of the knowledge of the glory of God in the face of Christ." (2 Corinthians 4:6)

❧ *I am the bride of Christ.* "Let us rejoice and be glad and give him glory! For the wedding of the Lamb has come, and his bride has made herself ready." (Revelation 19:7)

❧ *I am very bold.* "Since we have such a hope, we are very bold." (2 Corinthians 3:12) "Let us then approach the throne of grace with confidence, so that we may receive mercy and find grace to help us in our time of need." (Hebrews 4:16)

This isn't pop psychology. In the late nineteenth century, Hannah Whitall Smith wrote, "The things we think on are the things that feed the soul. If we think on pure and lovely things, we shall grow pure and lovely like them, and the converse is also true."[3] And Paul tells us to "take off your old self . . . and put on the new self which is being renewed in knowledge and in the image of its Creator" (Colossians 3:9-10, paraphrased). Once we are wooed by the truth and are present and aware of the knowledge it brings, God asks only one more thing of us — that we take time to rest and enjoy the beauty and freedom we have as his creation and simply believe it.

If you are like me and many other Christians, you may find it hard to leave the Wretch-Like-Me Club to join the Amazing-Grace Foundation. Like the woman at my business meeting, I sometimes fail to see myself living these words of truth. But if I return to the roots of my true identity and allow the Spirit to woo me to that truth to displace the lies, then I begin to find better ways to express it and ultimately to enjoy it. The truth revealed by the Spirit within me is a thing of beauty, the key to inspire my heart, to renew my mind, and to free my soul.

Break Through

1. Take time to come up with a truth statement about yourself using three adjectives and a noun. Turn this truth into prayer. Ask God to help you live this truth and claim, "I am that truth as God created me to be." Record your thoughts in your journal. Find another woman to share this exercise with and to pray for one another as you see how God transforms your lives.

2. How have you experienced truth in your own spiritual journey thus far? How have you covered up this truth in your life? Where do you need to experience Christ's truth as your new identity, to cast off the old harmful habits and to enrobe yourself in his beauty and tender thoughts toward you?

3. Consider the truth of your identity in Christ listed in the "Unearthing God's Liberating Truth" section. Which of these truths speak most powerfully into your heart today?

Meditate on how this truth changes or challenges your attitudes, actions, or belief system.

4. Revisit the Scripture and quotes at the beginning of the chapter. How does the quote by Craig Childs apply to truth in your own life? In the words of Teresa of Avila, how can you commit to "guard and nurture the soul's beauty" on a consistent basis? Write a prayer in response to these words.

Six

Break Through to Intimacy

All my longings lie open before you, O Lord; my sighing is not hidden from you.

Psalm 38:9

Why are you troubled, and why do doubts rise in your minds? Look at my hands and my feet. It is I myself! Touch me and see.

Luke 24:38-39

God is the Creator and the protector and the lover. For until I am substantially united to him, I can never have perfect rest or true happiness, until, that is, I am so attached to him that there can be no created thing between my God and me.

Julian of Norwich[1]

I've thought more about intimacy in the past few years than I have in all the combined minutes of my life thus far. I'm not sure if it's because I'm single again, or because I'm older, or because my children are older and leaving me more to myself. Regardless of the why, I'm hungry for intimacy, passionate about it, and homesick over it. Whenever I bring up the subject, I sense it makes a lot of folks uncomfortable, maybe puts them too close to their own gnawing emptiness.

Everyone has advice to help me handle this deep and universal hunger — or maybe it's just a ploy to get me to stop talking about it. They have thoughtful advice, such as, "Get a grip . . . get a man . . . get a life," or some such get-over-it response. But I'm not getting over it. In fact, I'm falling deeper into my desire for it. Maybe because intimacy is a key element to living a full life. The word *intimate* comes from the Latin *intimus*, which means "to make known or innermost." Webster defines intimacy as "one's deepest nature, essential, fundamental." And, indeed, intimacy is essential and fundamental to a meaningful life. If we go back to the creation of humanity, we can see this.

EXAMINING OUR RELATIONSHIPS

According to Scripture, God simply spoke the world — the sun, the moon, and the stars into existence. By the mere power of his thoughts, he created plants and animals in multitude. But when he designed humanity, he started with one and didn't just say, "Let there be man." Rather, God formed man with his own hands from the dust of the ground, and he did the same for woman. Then God stooped down and gave us that divine kiss, the breath of life. Our very creation was intimate, one on one, one by one. We were created with intimacy, with a touch and a kiss. We were created for intimacy with God and ultimately with each other.

I have my own ideas of what I expect from intimacy. Here's my definition: *To know and be known in a uniquely personal way, to love and be loved unconditionally, to touch and be touched with deep tenderness, compassion, and affection.* This is no easy definition to live out, because it requires vulnerability, and vulnerability risks being wounded in order to experience the joy of being loved. This is where we run into problems with intimacy. Our desire for intimacy may be from God, but we often flinch when touched by it, remembering past hurts delivered in the name of love. That's why it's important to examine how intimate we are in relationship to ourselves, others, and God.

Intimacy with self. If we are in touch with our "inmost place," our *inner being* that houses our "true north," our authentic, God-created self, we have intimacy with self. We know and love who God created us to be. Intimacy with self paves the way for intimacy with others and with God. If I can't be intimate with my inner self, then I'll have no capacity for intimacy with others or with God.

We lose touch with ourselves because it's much easier to let our inner being lie fallow than to plant and nurture and harvest truth. It's tempting to live a paved-over life, resurfaced by self-improvement, rather than to take time to intentionally examine our motives and actions, our convictions and commitments. As a result, our inmost being shrivels up due to neglect, leaving us spiritually undeveloped weaklings. But God encourages us over and over to look at our inner being and to allow him to care for it and feed it.

So I must look inward to prepare the ground of my heart, and I must look Godward to allow him to examine my heart, to search me and know my heart and lead me in the way I should go (Psalm 139:23-24). "All my longings lie open before you, O Lord; my sighing is not hidden from you" (Psalm 38:9). These intimate words encourage me to experiment with laying everything out on the table to God. This discipline is not so much to inform God of anything he doesn't already know, but rather to allow him to inform me about who I am in light of his grace.

Whether I write what I learn in a journal or offer it up as a prayer, God is hearing more from me these days about what's on my

mind and in my heart. That incessant internal stream of consciousness, even my physical desires and intimate fantasies, are finding
their way to God's heart. He's listening to why I find it unfair that
he calls me to be holy when it's unnatural for me to be so. He knows
when I resent giving up my personal time and when I'm fearful of
making a mess of my life. This open dialogue brings God into my
hidden parts and brings me into God's revealed heart.

Intimacy with others. For an introvert like me, it takes time and
attention for trust to grow to a point of intimacy with another
person. And for an extrovert, it may be more difficult to get past the
easy flow of, "Hi, how are you, let's do lunch," and delve more deeply
into really knowing and being known.

I recently attended a support-group counseling session with
my daughter. In a roomful of strangers I was shocked at how easily
everyone talked with each other about their heartaches. One woman
shared intimate details about her lifeless marriage and how she used
alcohol and illicit affairs to ease that pain. I felt embarrassed for her,
not realizing then how the act of confession allows us to empty our
pain to make room for new life and healing to occur.

Meanwhile, I felt all this raw, emotional openness as a near inva-
sion of privacy, and so I approached the group with a skeptic's heart
of judgment and came face-to-face with my fear of intimacy. When
it came my turn to share, I simply said, "I'll pass." And the group
moved on to the next addict. I saw how quickly I rejected intimacy
before it rejected me.

This encounter led me to consider (privately) with gut-wrenching
honesty the methods I use to avoid intimacy. Where do I hide
from intimacy? What are the masks I wear? At times I hide behind
my written words, or behind my independence and self-perceived
strength. I hide behind silence and even spiritual disciplines. When
I'm quick to judge another, I'm hiding from intimacy, because if I

can judge you before you judge me, then I don't have to trust you, or be hurt by you. Growing distrustful of others is great practice for growing distrustful of God.

Intimacy with God. The God "out there" is also the God who comes to us and pursues the heart willing to come to him. He came to us first in the Garden of Eden and walked with humanity. After sin and deception sent Adam and Eve into hiding, still God came and cried out for us through the thick separation that hung like a fog between him and his children. He came to Moses in a burning bush and to the wandering Israelites in a fiery cloud. He came to David through the prophet's words. He comes to us bodily through his people, the church. He comes to us visibly through all creation. Ultimately he came to the entire world through a baby in a manger, a touchable infant crying to be fed and held.

Despite God's desire to "know and be known" it's quite easy for us to avoid a real, intimate relationship with God, because it seems nearly impossible to cozy up to someone when that person is physically absent. So we say, "Why bother?" I even wonder if God can really meet my deepest longing when I'm yearning for a tender touch, a knowing smile, a loving embrace. But these are nothing more than the excuses of an "intimaphobic" like me.

I recently shared with my spiritual director my desire to experience intimacy with God more deeply and to reconnect with my hiding emotions more directly. She suggested that I offer this prayer and simply listen: *Lord, what are you inviting me to know, learn, or love in this place, time, circumstance, or emotion?*

This prayer often is simply a reminder of God's open invitation to be with him and rest in him. Other times I sense his thoughts breaking through my routines, such as when I took a lunch break in the garden of a nearby Franciscan retreat center. I brought my notes to work on my manuscript, but instead felt pulled by God's invitation to set it all aside and reconnect to him. I captured this thought in my journal:

A scent of mint, of wet earth, wakes my spirit. I look overhead through the leaves of the citrus trees and watch the clouds pass by. I nestle into a bent-wood chair and am mindful of the differences between this earthy shelter and the smooth glass and synthesized surfaces of my office. I pay attention to the reality living in the earth surrounding me beyond my scheduled, techno-savvy existence on the job. Time feels different here as well. Earth time, where leaves rustle to the rhythm of the wind and clouds make a leisurely, breathless path through the sky, reminds me that what I came here to do is overshadowed by the beauty of simply being — being ready and aware and present and prayerful, poised in anticipation of the Spirit's arrival and patient at heart as I wait for him.

These moments remind me that God is present. His name is *Emmanuel*, "God with us." He is around me. He is in me. And I am in him. There can be no closer, touchable connection than Spirit to spirit. Call it worship; call it prayer; call it meditation. All I know is that in such moments I am aware that I love and am loved, I know and am known, I touch and am touched by the nearness of God.

RESPONDING TO GOD'S INVITATION

Our desire to know God tells us we hunger for intimacy, but our life experience tells us to keep our distance for fear of yet another disappointing encounter. How compassionate and tender-hearted of God, knowing the dilemma of our inner struggle, to open the Upper Room meal with a reassurance that the time had come for Jesus to show us "the full extent of his love" (John 13:1).

So we come to him, conflicts and all. We come with skepticism, fear, schemes, and doubts. Even Judas was allowed to come to Jesus with his traitorous heart and to share bread and wine with the one he would eventually betray. We all come to the only one who can show us a fully extended love that never falls short of our hopes.

A dozen truths punch through that Upper Room scene, in particular God's relentless pursuit of us. Picking up a basin of water and a towel, Jesus kneels before the disciples (and us) and gently lifts their dirty feet into his strong hands and begins to wash away the dirt and massage away the hard calluses of their journey. Like most of the disciples, I'm left speechless when I stumble upon this scene; I'm jolted by this picture of God, who has all power and authority (John 13:3), choosing to be a humble servant (verses 4-5).

Peter gives voice to what most of us are thinking. He politely asks a question just to confirm his fear. "Lord, are you going to wash my feet?" (John 13:6). Peter's first reflex is to escape. After a gentle explanation from Jesus to relax and trust that it will all make sense one day, Peter comes back even stronger, "You will never wash my feet" (verse 8). To Peter's credit, I don't hear this as a prideful statement, as if he doesn't have any dirt on his feet, but rather as a realization that there is a gaping canyon between him and Christ, and Peter is on the wrong side of the canyon. He should be the one stooping at Jesus' feet. Peter had a similar escape response when Jesus first called him to be his disciple. "Go away from me, Lord; I am a sinful man!" (Luke 5:8).

How long has it been since I've let Jesus wash away the pain and soothe my tired spirit? How comfortable am I being comforted by the hands of Jesus? Yet, if I want to run away and escape this first step toward intimacy — letting Jesus wash away my pain and weariness — then I too will hear Jesus say, "Unless I wash you, you have no part with me" (John 13:8).

Next Peter tried to avoid intimacy by over-dramatizing and

over-inflating his desire to be closer to Christ than any other. Pride comes into the picture. "Lord, not just my feet, but anoint me more . . . cleanse me more . . . love me more than anyone else" (see verse 9). And now the one-on-one confrontation and intimate dialogue has turned into a "Hey-everybody-watch-me" kind of production. If Peter could avoid intimacy, then he wouldn't have to get down to the dirt on his feet.

I can relate to this response. Like King David, I see my sin because it's always before me (see Psalm 51:3). But even worse than the sin, is my lack of desire to do away with it. So I avoid Christ's touch. I'm suddenly too busy to open my Bible, too tired to pray, too strong-willed to humble myself and worship. I miss out on the face-to-face encounter with the true lover of my soul because I can't look him in the eye. I avoid intimacy when I pretend to dine with the Divine by diving deep into spiritual discipline, hoping my good habit will splash away the dust from the journey. But I only end up making mud puddles as I avoid the holy water held in Christ's basin that purifies my heart and sanctifies my path.

Thankfully, Jesus doesn't let Peter off the hook, and continues to pursue him, as he does us. After Peter's debate over the foot washing, Jesus reminds him he is already clean because he knows the whole-life saving grace for his soul.

Often in the step-by-step, everyday walk, we cry out for Christ's touch. We know the Savior of our lives, yet struggle with how to make him Lord of this minute. Every day we have those moments when we need to accept the invitation for Jesus to wash our feet.

That's what I needed yesterday morning on my way to work. I got stuck behind a driver going forty-five miles per hour in the fast lane of the freeway. My irritation turned to impatience and impatience grew to anger. Soon I began to honk at the man to move out of my way. Finally able to get around him, I honked one last time for good measure, glared at him and wondered, *what's his problem?*

I couldn't ignore the immediate thought that perhaps *I* was his problem. Perhaps his life had been one long season of dealing with people who refused to hold out grace when he was going as fast as he knew how to go. I was walking in the mire of the world, my steps out of sync with the Spirit. But, like Peter, I was now desperate and thankful all at once for the invitation from Christ to purify my feet, a symbolic point of contact between my saved soul and the real world. When I stop and set my feet into his outstretched hands, he hallows them and the ground where we walk, and prepares us for the journey ahead.

UNEARTHING GOD'S INTIMATE TOUCH

The image of Jesus washing my feet has become a picture of my intimacy with him as he teaches me to connect more intimately with others and to walk with them on their journey. And as I ask God what he is inviting me to know, to learn, and to love, he responds with the simple, intimate word, *Come.* "Come, let us reason together" (Isaiah 1:18). "Come, all you who are thirsty, come to the waters" (Isaiah 55:1). "Come to me . . . and I will give you rest" (Matthew 11:28). "Come with me by yourselves to a quiet place and get some rest" (Mark 6:31). My response to this invitation need not be complicated. I respond in kind with my own invitation to my Lord. And I pray, *Come, Lord Jesus* (Revelation 22:20).

I'm through thinking about intimacy — not because I've gotten over it, like some adolescent obsession. I'm done thinking about it logically because I'm falling deeper into it with my heart and spirit so that on occasion I'm actually living it and finding joy in drawing nearer to the Lover of my soul.

BREAK THROUGH

---

1. On a scale of 1-10, how comfortable are you with intimacy with others, with yourself, with God? When do you find yourself most longing for intimacy? Which tactics are you most prone to use when intimacy is offered: escape, avoidance, or acceptance?

2. Read John 13:1-17. Read it a second time more slowly. Listen to those words, phrases, or verses that pull at you or raise questions within you. Record those words in your journal and ask God to reveal himself through this dialogue. Now, place yourself at the table with the disciples. As Jesus approaches you with the basin and towel, what do you see? What shoes are you wearing? How are they a symbol of who you are? What does Jesus ask of you? How comfortable are you in placing your feet in Jesus' hands? How will you respond? Ask him to consecrate the footsteps of your physical, emotional, and spiritual journey that have led you to this point. Thank him for his promise to lead you in the future. But above all, ask him for the vision to see the place where you stand at this moment as the rich soil found in the holy ground of intimate communion with him.

3. Read Matthew 11:28-29. In your journal, rewrite Christ's invitation as if he were personally writing to you. (For example, "Dear Marsha, come to me and rest from . . .") After you have written and received Jesus' invitation, write your RSVP response to his words. Be honest and open as you respond to him.

4. Revisit the quotes at the beginning of this chapter. Consider
    the Luke 24 Scripture. How do these words speak to the
    heart, the body, and the spirit all at once? Write a prayer in
    response to these words.

SEVEN

BREAK THROUGH TO PASSION

Awake my soul! . . . for great is your love, reaching to the heavens; your faithfulness reaches to the skies.

PSALM 57:8,10

Because of the LORD's great love we are not consumed, for his compassions never fail. They are new every morning; great is your faithfulness.

LAMENTATIONS 3:22-23

It is not so much you praying to God, but God praying in you . . . it is the time given, the willingness to turn the Word and the Voice loose in us. It is the willingness to listen to the scriptures and the saints and even the sound of our own innermost being, the being into which God has whispered things that no one else will ever hear. It is the willingness to let the Word form us rather than always being content with or insisting upon what we can dig out with our own intellect and understanding.

ROBERT BENSON[1]

I mark the mid-eighties as a turning point in my spiritual life and my relationship with God. This was a time when I reevaluated the Christian *lifestyle* I'd grown up with and felt Christ himself drawing me to his side. I sensed he was asking me personally, "Do you love me — beyond the church activity, the Bible study lessons, the Sunday potluck — do you love me? During this time I seemed to wake up in more ways than one. It wasn't a rude awakening, but more of a gentle spiritual awakening to an awareness of God speaking to me in personal ways and reassuring me of his presence through my everyday life.

While God's been known to shout his messages through mighty voices of the ancient prophets, more often he speaks to me in quiet thoughts, prompting me to notice subtle beauty and his ordinary offerings of grace in the daily rhythm of life. God's movement awakened many things in me, but three awakenings in particular profoundly changed my life and remain fresh on my mind today. They make me aware of how God uses the most creative ways to reach each individual heart.

The first awakening occurred with the birth of my children, as those bedazzling feelings of parental love nearly knocked me to my knees in wonder. I'm certain most parents experience this, whether it be their first or fifth child. A love I never knew existed was suddenly alive within me and created a fierce and undying bond of devotion to my children. It reached deep-seated instinct and at the same time a spiritual realm of divine delight that connected me to the father-love of God toward me, his child.

Along with this new parental love, I also became aware of a compelling urge to write. This was my second awakening. Writing had never been my habit or desire in the past, so I can point only to God's movement within me that prompted me to pick up pen and paper and give it a try. My writing wasn't beautiful stuff, not great stuff, but raw, rough writing that helped me find my voice and discover over time who I am. In my journals I captured my moods, my questions and truths, my grocery lists, my challenges and fears, my loves, my longings, my sorrows and hopes. Through writing I settled into my own skin and finally felt at home with me.

Around this same time I experienced my third awakening: I discovered the classic writings of the Christian faith. I nearly devoured the lives of these saints whose ardor and undying passion for Christ painted graphic visions of how I too might fall more deeply in love with my Savior — Augustine, Luther, Julian of Norwich, St. Benedict, Thomas à Kempis, and more contemporary pilgrims, such as Thomas Merton, Henri Nouwen, Dietrich Bonhoeffer, and Richard Foster. While reading their books, I began to open my Bible to read along with them. New thoughts and ideas emerged. Stories and verses I'd known and memorized in childhood grabbed me in a new way and spoke to me in the circumstance and struggles I was facing at that particular season of life. I responded to it all through more writing. I couldn't let the gift of God's gentle voice slip through my mind without giving it a place to rest on the pages of my journal.

All these awakenings were no coincidence. I experienced them more as a majestic symphony orchestrated and conducted by God. He stirred within me a love for his faithful presence, spoken in profound experiences like childbirth, in the simple beauty of a wildflower, or in a multitude of voices descending down to me through the centuries. This newfound passion did not occur like a lightbulb going off in my mind, as if I finally "got it." Rather it has been like the sun rising within me each day. The wonder of it all is that the newness has never left me, and it's now over two decades later.

I'd be lying if I said I haven't had stretches when I felt distant from God, such as I felt when I became aware of that emotional disconnect I mentioned in the first chapter. But never have I doubted God's presence that stirs my heart to passion, and this is why I could pray for *renewed* passion at that season of my life. In fact, the desire to know God, to listen for his voice, and to follow his lead only intensifies during those times. So while life and emotion and circumstance constantly move me from one transition to the next, God always remains faithfully whispering his love through the Spirit's voice, awakening my desire to passionately follow him.

FINDING THE PATH TO PASSION

The more time I dwell with Christ and in the Word of God, the easier it becomes to recognize and respond to God's voice. But it takes a developed discipline not only to learn to listen, but to *want* to listen and connect with him. Three paths have led me to more consistently remain in dialogue with God. This is the most natural method I know to developing a life of unceasing prayer, where spiritual passion is kindled.

I first came upon these three paths through one of my favorite authors, the late Henri Nouwen, priest and spiritual counselor to countless millions through his writings to this generation of seekers. He marked the way to hearing God's voice as follows:[2]

- *Listen to the Living Word* through the life of Jesus.
- *Respond to God's voice* through the discipline of journaling.
- *Meditate on the written Word* through the discipline of *lectio divina* (sacred reading).

These are three distinct paths, yet they often merge into one avenue toward knowing God. I can listen to the Living Word (Christ) only when informed from the written Word (Scripture), and I can respond to what God is saying to me only when I'm immersed in meditative reading of the Word.

Listen to the Living Word through the life of Jesus. It's so important, that in coming to the written Holy Scriptures we never forget to listen to the Living Word, that name given to Christ. Jesus himself warns us to not stop short at reading the Word. "You diligently study the Scriptures because you think that by them you possess eternal life. These are the Scriptures that testify about me, yet you refuse to come to me to have life" (John 5:39-40).

The written Word confirms that the Living Word, Jesus, gives life through a creative process. "If anyone is in Christ, he is a new creation" (2 Corinthians 5:17). When Mary listened to God's voice expressed through the angel, she responded, "May it be to me as you have said" (Luke 1:38). She entered into the great agreement to join God in the act of creation and was forever changed in the process. He invites us to this same partnership through creative, transforming acts of renewal in the places where we live our ordinary lives. Let me show you what I mean.

One late afternoon several years ago, I ate a sandwich in a large but empty fast-food dining room. I thanked God for the space and the peace and quiet in my busy day. Then an elderly woman came in, ordered her sandwich, and chose to sit in the booth directly behind me so that we were sitting back to back in an enormously large and empty room. She ate loudly, smacking her lips and slurping her soda, and I quickly lost my appetite and could feel irritation rising in me. She left quickly, and I returned to my solitude, but only for a few moments.

Next came a homeless man. Immediately my thoughts put up walls between us as I mentally willed him to *sit over there on the other side of the room*. The odor of his unwashed body arrived before he did as he chose a table three steps away from mine. Again, I looked around the room wondering why he had to "cozy up" to my space with his dirty bags and his mumbling stream of consciousness. I couldn't take it. I gathered my purse and tray and quickly escaped into the fresh air. I realized I forgot my drink on the table but figured the man would take advantage of a free refill so I left it there — a grand act of compassion.

It wasn't until later that evening that I processed what had happened. My first thoughts were self-recriminating, wondering why I hadn't at least acknowledged these strangers and welcomed them in some way — smiled, engaged in conversation, offered to buy a meal for the man. Guilt began its destructive work when suddenly the loving voice of the Living Word broke through my mumbling stream of guilt. *Don't you see that these people chose to draw close to you because I am alive in you. Why wouldn't they want to be near you?*

In this realization I was re-created and transformed. Christ was inviting me to leave the guilt-trip and to see myself as a vessel of his divine purpose, even when my thoughts take me far away from that reality. To such an invitation I respond with passion, "May it be to me as you have said." That moment, that event, those words from Christ, changed me. I make it a point to look strangers in the eye, to smile and greet those I encounter. I pray blessings of peace over individuals I see walking on the street or waiting at the bus stop and enter into that great agreement to join God in his creative acts of renewal.

This is how Jesus, the Living Word, speaks to us. In listening for his voice we communicate to God our willingness to be teachable, and in this posture of sitting at Jesus' feet we are re-created and passion is restored. As Nouwen puts it, "the full power of the word lies not in how you apply it to your life after you have heard it but in how its transforming power does its divine work in you as you listen."[3]

Respond to God's voice through journaling. According to Socrates, "An unexamined life is not worth living." Certainly there are many ways to examine a life, but for me journaling has become a well-worn path to finding God, listening to his voice, and finding passion. It is no coincidence that *journal* and *journey* derive from the same root word that Webster defines as "a place of progress." My journal is more than just the place to capture what I've experienced or observed today. My journal is where discovery *begins*, where I pay attention to the word that God is writing on my heart. I like how Michel de Montaigne, a French writer from the seventeenth century, explains it, "I write to paint myself. There is no one who, if he listens to himself, does not discover in himself a pattern all his own."[4]

Several things happen when we journal. First, writing slows the heart and thought patterns to allow real meaning to surface. Humans speak conversationally at a rate of 180-220 words per minute. We can type (depending on our skill level) at around 50-100 words a minute. But we write at approximately 30-40 words per minute. The world operates at a frenetic pace. (I discovered *frenetic* comes from a Latin word that means brain disease.) God's timing and pace may require that I slow down, breathe, imagine, contemplate, and rest in his Word in order to heal the brain disease. "His quiet performances are indirect, deep, serene, and seemingly slow and have to be explored to be understood and appreciated. . . . He is continually winning the battle in quiet, circuitous ways."[5] And while "slow" may seem the diametric opposite of "passionate," it's often in this relaxed pace where we break through to "aha" moments that quicken our spirits and ignite new ideas even in the midst of the mundane.

I spent one Sunday morning reflecting on where I was at in my relationship with God in my ordinary daily life, and recorded this prayer in my journal:

I think we're more relaxed in this relationship of ours, Lord, in the sense of my being more authentic with you, of being okay when the rhythms of my life change due to demands of work or relationships. I know in the core of my being that our connection is not broken by anything so petty as how I exercise my habit of devotion. I've seen you in unexpected places and in conversations I never dreamed of having with people I never dreamed of meeting. I've seen you shine through my life even when I'm not trying to "polish you up" and make you presentable or palatable to the world. I've seen you in my struggles over the choices I make on any given day, wanting to please you, wondering if what I'm doing does please you, and in that struggle knowing that I'm missing the fact that you simply delight in me. This is how and where I want to grow, because the more fully I experience your delight, the more I'll find delight in living this life with passion.

Journaling is the discipline whereby I stay present and current with God. In the present moment he reveals his thoughts even as he helps to clarify my thoughts. There is no magic in this. But it has become a practice where I invite my mental, physical, emotional, social, and spiritual dimensions to dance with the divine on the tip of my pen. Sometimes the dance is a jitterbug, sometimes a Viennese waltz, other times just a swaying embrace. The Living Word invites me to respond as I spin my prayer on the pages of my journal.

Meditate on the written Word. I recently learned that the Hebrew word for meditate, *hagah*, is the same word translated as *growl*, as a lion growls over its food. This gives me a deeper sense of what it means to meditate over God's Word, making it the object of my hunger and passion, putting teeth into it, consuming it, making it mine so it becomes a part of me. This is what has been called through the ages *lectio divina*, or sacred reading. This way of reading Scripture gives new meaning to the words, "Taste and see that the LORD is good" (Psalm 34:8).

This past year I've meditated on the prayer that Paul penned in his letter to the Ephesian church: "I pray that you being rooted

and established in love, may have the power . . . to grasp how wide
and long and high and deep is the love of Christ . . . that you may be
filled to the measure of all the fullness of God" (Ephesians 3:17-19).
I'm awed by this prayer and by the possibility of being filled with
God's fullness. That single word *fullness* often rises as a two-syllable
centering prayer throughout my day, and I'm exploring new images
of what God has in mind for me when I pray this passage.

But I find it difficult to imagine the glory of knowing God in his
fullness in the midst of my ongoing distractions and stresses, challenges and obstacles. So I posed this question to God as I meditated
on his fullness: *What do you want me to comprehend about your immense
and immeasurable fullness, Lord?* As soon as I offered this question, my
thoughts shifted. Perhaps I don't need to see to the edge of eternity
to understand the fullness of God. Maybe I simply need to start
at this moment. While God's fullness exists beyond any earthly
dimension, the reference to width and length, height and depth,
implies a *measurable* fullness in *human* terms.

When I think of width or breadth, I imagine that moment of
birth when the nurse measures the circumference of a baby's head,
and I think of how God fills the mind with his love. And the baby's
length from head to toe is filled with godly intentions. The height of
human life is expressed in the stature of divine character. The depth
is the measure of God's full compassion that plumbs the deep emotions, pains and aches for wholeness as "deep calls to deep." When
I meditate on the Word of God in this way, it has the capacity to
live in me and to reveal the measure of God's fullness within me. I
need not struggle to know the immensity of God, except within the
constraints of my own common life.

UNEARTHING GOD'S VOICE

I have yet to "have my fill" of listening for the voice of God, for in it I learn to live with passion. His Word invites me to draw from an ever-flowing stream of life. Some days I take in long passages of Scripture, enjoying the plots of God's storyline running through the history of humanity. Other days I find a simple word or phrase that feeds me as an ongoing prayer for days on end.

Do I always hear God's voice? No. Do I always know the "answer" to whatever is troubling me? Not always. Do I correctly discern the way God is leading through a difficult stretch of life? Often I'm confused, or feel lost, or frustrated. But this I can claim: Always God speaks, hoping to stir our hearts to passion through soul-waking wonder, such as the birth of a child or a new attitude toward life. Each new day, new transition, or a new challenge is an invitation to listen and respond and meditate in the rhythm and language of unceasing praise. While we grow in our ability and desire to hear God's voice, he never stops revealing ordinary offerings of grace that whisper his name. He is perpetually filling us and waking us to a life of meaning and passion so that we can respond, "May it be to me as you have said."

BREAK THROUGH

1. In what ways have you been most aware of God speaking or reaching to you throughout your life? What has God been speaking to you about most recently? How are you responding? In what ways do you sense a waking passion or strong desire to pursue or explore something new? What might God be telling you about that passion?

2. Which of the three paths to passion have you traveled the most frequently — listening to the Living Word, responding to God's voice through journaling, or meditating on the written Word? Which are you most interested in exploring? Find one other woman willing to explore and experiment in unearthing God's faithfulness by developing a regular habit of devotion and then sharing together your experience on a weekly basis.

3. Integrate all three of the paths to hearing God's voice — listening, responding, meditating — by reading one of the following passages of Scripture: Mark 14:1-11; Luke 1:26-38; Luke 12:1-34; Luke 13:10-17. Or choose your own passage of Scripture from the life of Jesus.

   Now, come to God, asking him to quiet your heart. Take a couple of deep breaths as a way to inhale his peace and exhale your distractions. Breathe in his stillness; release your busyness. When you feel your mind and muscles begin to relax, begin to read the chosen Scripture. Don't read it with the intention of figuring it out or studying it. Come with no agenda or expectation. Come only in simple faith, willing to listen. Read the verses once. Go back and read it a second time more slowly. You may want to read it aloud a third time. As you read, pay attention to words or phrases that strike a chord within you. Rest on those words. Remain in Jesus and his words to you. Ask any question that enters your thoughts and then listen.

   If you're new to meditating on the Word, don't worry if you don't sense anything right away. Come back to the Scripture passage again, later in the day or throughout the week. Continue to be open to God's voice. Over time, new insights may appear, or tender impressions of who God is in light of these words. Record your experience, your response, your desire, your prayer after you've spent your time in the Word.

4. Revisit the Scriptures and quotation at the beginning of this chapter. Respond to these words in your journal.

EIGHT

BREAK THROUGH TO GRACE

Let the peace of Christ rule in your hearts since . . . you were called to peace. Let the word of Christ dwell in you richly . . . with gratitude in your hearts to God. . . . Let your conversation be always full of grace.

COLOSSIANS 3:15-16; 4:6

It is good for our hearts to be strengthened by grace.

HEBREWS 13:9

Lord, make me an instrument of Your peace; where there is hatred, let me sow love; where there is injury, pardon, where there is doubt, faith; where there is despair, hope; where there is darkness, light; and where there is sadness, joy. O Divine Master, grant that I may not so much seek to be consoled as to console; to be understood as to understand; to be loved as to love; for it is in giving that we receive, it is in pardoning that we receive pardon, and it is in dying that we are born to eternal life.

ST. FRANCIS OF ASSISI [1]

I was having coffee with a friend who was struggling with what she wanted to do with her life, wondering if God had a specific purpose for her. We had had this conversation before, but at times my friend gets stuck in negative self-talk, believing old lies that tell her she can't do what she wants to do, which keeps her from moving forward. The more she talked, the more irritated I became with my talented, beautiful, giving friend, and I told her so. "Why do you do that?" I asked. "Why do you put yourself down and feel sorry for yourself? Why don't you just step out and try something, anything? There's no right or wrong answer here. . . ." On and on I unloaded all my impatient, frustrated "advice." When I finally took a breath, I realized she was near tears, with a look that said, "Thanks for the encouragement."

She told me later that she felt as if she was going to have a panic attack right there at Starbucks. It made me realize that sometimes my words and my life fail to display the grace of God at work in me. In fact, my words have the potential to bury grace beneath harsh rebuffs.

I was six years old when I first learned that words have the power to create or destroy life. My dear first grade teacher consoled a child on her lap and then looked at the rest of the class and matter-of-factly explained, "Children, when you say something to someone, whether good words or bad, you can't take it back. Once the words are said, they can't be erased." We simply sat in silence with her wisdom. For some reason, maybe because of my love for words, that moment left an indelible memory in my mind.

I've always been careful with my words, and so I'm asking myself why, in recent years, I've lost some of that careful respect for the mystery of the spoken word. As much as I want my words to be enlightened and encouraging and exceptional, I've sensed that hard-hearted, graceless attitude escaping from my lips more often than I'd like to admit. So I continue to pray and ask God to guard my tongue and to be the gatekeeper of my words while he forms my heart with his kindness.

GROWING IN GRACE

What we say and do is an outward expression of what's in our hearts. Even when we try to say the right thing, a certain tone or expression may convey a message of impatience or judgment. When we speak, what's inside can rise to the surface in bursts of defensiveness or too-loud demands. Sometimes I try to be funny with my words, but I regret at what price the laughter comes. This is where God's grace must grow inside of me, because until I know grace deep down for myself, I cannot speak it into the hearts of others.

The writer of Hebrews tells us, "See to it that no one misses the grace of God" (12:15). This is a noble calling; one worthy of our efforts to understand what it means. We know that God's grace is his unconditional and unmerited kindness toward us. Grace is offered to us through Christ's death on the cross. It pays the punishment for our sin. It reopens the doorway that allows us to enter the Holy of Holies and know God in his fullness. It brings us back into favor with God as his beloved children. All this is accomplished for us while we are weak sinners, unable to earn such a gift by our own efforts.

God's great kindness saves us, but his grace also continues to grow within us as we devote ourselves to nurturing that gift in our daily lives, our conversations, our relationships, and our work. So while we can never earn extra measures of grace (it's already given in full), we do have the ability to access it and live more deeply within it, to allow it to inform our words and actions every day. In Paul's letter to the Colossian church, he offers pithy reminders of how to live in grace: "Set your hearts on things above . . . rid yourself of . . . anger, rage, malice, slander . . . bear with each other . . . let the peace of Christ rule in your hearts . . . let the word of Christ dwell in you richly . . . devote yourselves to prayer, being watchful and thankful . . . make the most of every opportunity . . . let your conversations be always full of grace" (Colossians 3:1,8,13,15-16; 4:2,5-6).

The question is: How? How do I avoid conversations like the one I had with my friend in the coffee shop where my words lack the kindness of grace? How do I grow in grace and avoid the common problem of taking it for granted? I believe three disciplines of the heart help to cultivate and experience the wonder of grace in our own lives. As a result, grace will more consistently overflow into other lives. These are the disciplines of silence, generosity, and gratitude. All three disciplines work to empty our souls of everything that hinders the growth of grace to make room for the nurturing kindness of our loving God.

THE DISCIPLINE OF SILENCE

Our culture bombards us with words until they become nothing more than incessant noise. We add to that noise when we join the throngs of people who are too quick to speak, to make their point, to demand their rights, to be heard and justified. But we can learn to live in grace and offer it to others through practicing the discipline of silence. In silence we learn to listen, to wait on the Lord, to relinquish our control, and to trust that he is present and working. "Be still, and know that I am God" (Psalm 46:10). When I offer up silence as a prayer, I make space in my otherwise noisy, demanding world for God to speak. I give up my controlling habits to ease my heartache or to make people respond to me in certain ways, and to protect my own reputation.

Silence invites grace to break through within us in the following ways:

It calms. On most days the first two or three hours of my morning are an offering of silence to God. It has become easier to find silence as I've gotten older and my family has grown more independent. But regardless of seasons of life, I believe God calls us to find that quiet time to be alone with him, whether for ten minutes or two hours or an entire day. I'm not talking about sitting and staring into silent space. It may be reading, thinking, writing, praying, walking, watching the sunrise, drinking coffee, or getting ready for work. In such stillness we become aware of the Spirit working in our inner being.

It's not always possible, but whenever I'm alone, I try to avoid filling the silence with pointless noise. I become aware of the still and quiet presence of God and ask him to refill my spirit with his grace. Isaiah reminds us that in rest and quietness we find strength, but we often lack the desire to pursue quietness or create space for silence. It may even seem like an exercise in boredom, but there's nothing boring about God's promise when we enter into his sanctuary of quietness. "In repentance and rest is your salvation, in quietness and trust is your strength, but you would have none of it . . . yet the Lord longs to be gracious to you; he rises to show you compassion . . . . Blessed are all who wait for him!" (Isaiah 30:15,18).

This discipline of silence has been my great comfort when I've struggled with those inner voices and the rush of thoughts that silently scream demands and fears, or whisper disappointments and doubts into my life. How do we truly enter that stillness where we know that "he is God"? I sometimes find relief by envisioning those taunting accusations and lies as a stream of words flowing past me on their way to the throne of God. My mind calms as I let thoughts and distractions pour into God's sea of stillness, and I enter the rehabilitating, calming grace of God's quiet presence.

It communicates kindness. Not only can silence refresh and calm us, it is also a powerful tool in how we communicate. Just as the psalms call us to praise and lift our voices, they often stop us in mid-thought with the one-word invitation: *Selah* — be still and think. The word itself sounds like a breath, a sigh, a reminder to slow down and be present with the word of God. In this way our dialogue with God becomes as natural as breathing, a taking in and giving out. Just as words on a page cannot be understood without the contrasting white space between them and between the sentences, so too, what is spoken is often understood in the space of what is left unsaid. Silence invites God's grace and kindness to sink deep into our souls.

I knew a youth pastor who spent hours on the basketball court every week with a group of streetwise teenage boys. One day, a church member observed the interaction between the youth leader and the boys. The young men's foul language didn't seem to faze the pastor, nor did he address it as a problem with them. The church member asked the pastor, "Why don't you confront these guys about their offensive language. Have you shared the gospel of Jesus with them yet?"

The pastor smiled and quietly responded, "I can't speak the gospel until I can live the gospel with these guys. When they know me and see Christ at work in me, maybe they'll open the door and maybe then I'll have something to say." This pastor knew the power of speaking out of silence. He knew he need not try to control the outcome or behavior of others when God was at work in their midst. Even in his conversation, he practiced silence as a means of inviting God to use him. It became an act of kindness and unconditional love toward these boys, but also an act of kindness to God himself as he invited him to speak. When we're filled up by God's kindness through the discipline of silence, we then have the resources to be "poured out," as we become generous of heart.

THE DISCIPLINE OF GENEROSITY

One of my favorite verses in the New Testament is 2 Corinthians 9:8. It says, "And God is able to make all grace abound to you, so that in all things at all times, having all that you need, you will abound in every good work." I like these words for two reasons: First, they leave no loopholes in our ability to experience grace, as the verse covers every season and circumstance and ends by making our good works abound. But I also like it because the promise comes, surprisingly as a result of our generous giving (verses 6-7). Don't misunderstand. This is not saying we can earn grace, but rather it outlines the way to experience the grace already given.

I was fortunate to see the connection between grace and generosity modeled through the life of my father who was the most generous man I've known. He was never wealthy, but he was always giving. He held his possessions loosely in his hands, knowing they were gifts on loan from God to be used for his good purposes. Dad's home, his cars, his time, his money, his affection, his laughter were God's tools for ministry. I never saw him give grudgingly. He seemed to consider it a privilege. I heard him say to so many people, "Keep it as long as you need it. . . . consider it your own. . . . I wish I had more to give." Although I can't recall a specific example, I'm sure some people may have taken advantage of his generous heart. But it never seemed to hinder his giving.

I know my father's graciousness was from God, but I believe it grew as a result of times when he was in need and became the recipient of generosity from others. He often told the story of when he moved our family to a new town so he could attend seminary. We arrived with little money. But a family friend stood in the town square, waiting for us, and gave my dad not much more than $100 to get us on our feet. That gift (along with my dad's willingness to humble himself to accept it) seemed to open his heart to expressing God's grace in similar ways. When I read Paul's words about grace and giving, I see my dad:

> *You will be made rich in every way so that you can be generous on every occasion, and through us your generosity will result in thanksgiving to God. This service that you perform is not only supplying the needs of God's people but is also overflowing in many expressions of thanks to God. . . . And in their prayers for you their hearts will go out to you, because of the surpassing grace God has given you. Thanks be to God for this indescribable gift!* (2 Corinthians 9:11-12, 14-15)

And when thanksgiving like this becomes our habit, we begin to experience how the discipline of gratitude moves us deeper into grace.

THE DISCIPLINE OF GRATITUDE

In the mid eighties I learned the discipline of the "God Hunt" from the ministry of David and Karen Mains.[2] Through this exercise I intentionally trained my heart to recognize and record occurrences of God at work in my everyday life. While I haven't maintained a daily log of "God sightings," my journal entries throughout the years remind me of his presence and involvement. These moments of gratitude roll out the red carpet for grace to enter in. Here are some of my notes of gratitude from the past month.

- Ryan and Alexandra's wedding day . . . tears of joy over their unity in Christ, the future set before them, and a love to grow within them.

- Learning the difference between being an information seeker and a wisdom seeker.
- The joy on my daughter Amy's face as we celebrated her life and high school graduation with family and friends.
- A break-through thought on a difficult topic helps me open up and communicate my heart.
- The gorgeous Mexican Bird of Paradise planted by the roadside for miles along the freeway creates a solid wall of orange blooms on my way to work.

With each awareness of God's hand, I offer a prayer of thanksgiving. This discipline of seeking God and responding with gratitude keeps me connected to his continual offerings of grace.

I've thought more than once about how the conversation with my friend at Starbucks might have gone differently if I had allowed gratitude to guide my words. I would have told her how grateful I am for her example of how to seek after God in all she does. I would have reminded her that her spirit of hospitality shines through her life wherever she goes. Such grace would have encouraged her and helped her see God at work in her. She and I both would have left in peace rather than a panic. But grace never lives out of regrets that wish to redo what I've already done. That's why I'm most grateful that my friend lives in God's grace too, and offers it to me when I'm in my most irritable, frustrated state of mind. In gratitude grace grows.

UNEARTHING GOD'S COMPASSIONATE KINDNESS

The compassionate kindness of God breaks through our lives through these three disciplines that ask us to empty ourselves in order to be filled. In this emptiness, the poor in spirit become rich, indescribably rich as heirs to the kingdom of God. In silence, we release the fear-filled need to control and we trust God's grace to speak. In our generosity, we release our grip on worldly desires and take hold of heaven's riches. And in our gratitude, we release those haunting regrets and move with confidence because despite our way with words, God continually strengthens our hearts with his grace.

BREAK THROUGH

1. In what ways have you seen or experienced grace as a practical act of kindness?

2. What is your experience or attitude toward the discipline of silence? When has silence cleared the ground for you to think more clearly or sense God more keenly? In what ways do you practice silence in an ordinary week? If silence is not a natural part of your day, what changes might you make to incorporate a little quietness into your routine?

3. If you could weigh the levels of gratitude and frustration in your life, which way would the scale tip? Choose one or more of the following exercises to help develop an awareness and habit of thanksgiving. Integrate this discipline into your daily life. Be mindful of how the discipline of gratitude is nurturing grace with you. Record your observations at the end of each week.

   ❧ Read Psalm 103, which is a song of praise listing the benefits of knowing God. Rewrite this psalm as a prayer of gratitude. Meditate on these benefits every morning.

   ❧ Develop the "God Hunt" discipline with another person or at mealtime with your family, and share how you saw

God at work in your life today. Record your God sightings in a notebook and give thanks for the acts of kindness direct from the hand of God.

  ❦   Thank people every day for what they've done, for who
they are, for the difference they make in your life. Write
thank-you cards at the end of each week to those individuals who have had an impact on your life.

4. For a twenty-four hour period of time, record every act of
generosity, great or small, that is offered to you and every act
of generosity that you offer to others. Read the prayer of St.
Francis at the beginning of the chapter as a reminder of how
we give and receive generously. Choose a word or phrase from
this prayer and make it your breath prayer, a phrase that you
offer frequently throughout the day and as a reminder to live
in the generosity of grace.

5. Revisit the Scriptures and quotation at the beginning of this
chapter. Reflect on these words in your journal.

NINE

BREAK THROUGH TO LOVE

Your kingdom come, your will be done on earth as it is in heaven.

MATTHEW 6:10

It is God's will that you should be sanctified.

1 THESSALONIANS 4:3

Every moment and every event of every man's life on earth plants something in his soul. For just as the wind carries thousands of winged seeds, so each moment brings with it germs of spiritual vitality that come to rest imperceptibly in the minds and wills of men. . . . Most of these unnumbered seeds perish and are lost, because men are not prepared to receive them, for such seeds as these cannot spring up anywhere except in the good soil of freedom, spontaneity and love.

THOMAS MERTON[1]

More than any other matter of faith, we Christians struggle with discerning God's will in our lives. We grapple with it for many reasons, but for most of us, I believe, it is an honorable struggle driven by our desire to love God with our heart, soul, mind, and strength. It's just that we get hung up, wishing for a checklist to determine if we're living up to that desire.

I know, because I spent many hours exploring how we can determine God's will in the way we act, the way we think, and in our attitudes toward our physical existence. I wondered about God's will in the realm of work, money, and relationships. I wanted to put my finger on a simple code of conduct or rule of life that would make it easy to figure out God's will and way of love as opposed to my own will and way of self-pleasing.

However, the harder I tried to get my mind around it all, the more frustrated I became in discerning God's direction. Round and round I went until I was dizzy following paths that took me nowhere. I ultimately concluded that what I understood about myself and about God's will was . . . absolutely nothing!

Still in turmoil about how to determine God's will, I put on my tennies, and set out to walk. As I walked, a prayer that my daughter had shared with me from her AA group came to mind. She called it the "set aside" prayer. *Lord, help me set aside everything I know about ___ ___.* I remember asking her, "What's the rest of it? Isn't there something else? 'Help me set aside what I know about _____, so that I can understand something or do something?'" She shook her head and said, "No, Mommy. That's it. Just, 'help me set aside what I know about _____.'"

So that's what I did on this day of frustration. I said the words aloud as I walked, *Lord, help me set aside everything I know about your will. Period. Amen.* At first I struggled to make it be something more, and I sensed how much I strain to make things happen, to produce a clever thought, to discover a new idea or truth.

That prayer helped me relax. I walked, not with thoughts of trying to get to an answer, or even trying to get a good workout. I simply walked at a comfortable stride without accusing myself of wasting time and allowing the exercise to lift my spirits and give me a new point of view in communicating God's will.

BATTLE OF THE WILLS

The battle of living in God's will takes place in the earthly realities of the daily grind. We pray until we're blue in the face about where to live, what job to take, whom to marry, how to deal with difficult people, what to do with unhealthy habits, and how to live with ourselves when we seem to make no progress in our battles to overcome. Even Jesus' model prayer addresses the battle to connect God's will in heaven to our reality on earth, "Your will be done on earth as it is in heaven" (Matthew 6:10). What do we mean when we speak of God's will? His will is his pleasure, his purpose, his intention, and his preference. As I've "set aside what I know about God's will," he's paved new paths to understand what that means for me.

God's will does not guarantee a certain and "successful" outcome. Even when I choose God's way, I still must examine where that path leads me. For instance, when I first started writing over twenty years ago, I felt God's incredible pleasure upon me as I did so. I never doubted that it was his will that I express myself in this way. I never doubted that he would use this delightful gift for the good of his people. I never doubted that his will was that my writing minister to others. Yet, as I continued in his will, I slowly began to turn the gift itself into the object of my affection.

Ultimately, I felt God calling me to set aside my misplaced love of writing and redirect it back to the Giver of that gift. I rebelled. I didn't want to give up this pleasure, but God had asked me to make a choice: I could either try to justify the way I idolized my writing, or I could put down my pen so I could hold God's hand and walk with him on my journey. So I laid it all down with the knowledge that God might never release me to pick it up again, and with the acceptance that I might never again experience that pleasure if I continued to value it over God. I got rid of anything related to writing, including my journal, and even my writing magazines. For over a year I relearned how to relate to God, to pray without a pen in my hand, to enjoy God's presence and sense his pleasure upon me through the beauty of his creation or in loving my children.

All this to explain that when I acted according to the will of God, it didn't turn out the way I expected, because I was defining God's will by worldly standards of success within a chosen vocation. This was my first clue that God's will is not a specific task or career or calling. *God's will is that I seek after and love him first, not second or third or somewhere down the line of priorities.* He promises that when we love him above all else, other things will be given to us as well (see Matthew 6:33). This is what happened to me. After rediscovering my ability to enjoy my relationship with God, I was able to come to him with my writing as an expression of our mutual devotion to one another. This helped me come to the next new understanding of his will.

God's will is not black and white, true or false, right or wrong. Unfortunately some Christians present themselves (and Christ) to the world as judges. Jesus said, "I did not come to judge the world, but to save it" (John 12:47). Yet some use arm-twisting tactics to coerce others into following Jesus at a certain time and in a certain manner. In doing so, they often shut the door of love to so many others. They pull up God's welcome mat and mis-shape his Word into artillery to defend their own cause.

Of course, I'm not talking here about issues of social justice.

Jesus himself said he was sent to proclaim freedom for the prisoners and to release the oppressed (see Luke 4:18). That is a clear indication of his will. However, when we step into God's will for the sake of promoting our own cause, we often forget that Christ also calls us to love our enemies (see Luke 6:27).

"Find out what pleases the Lord" (Ephesians 5:10). Paul's words imply that there isn't a list to choose from to get involved in God's will. Such a belief turns the mystery of divine love into mundane rules of conduct.

In the film *Chocolat*, we see two characters — one who lives by the code of law in his role as City Magistrate, the other who lives by the code of love in her chocolate shop. While many of the villagers see the chocolate as sinful temptation, the shopkeeper creates a place of refuge and encouragement for the downtrodden and outcast. In her shop we see people laughing, working, weeping, and living life with passion. In the town hall we see them worrying, getting sick, and living in frustration and fear.

It doesn't take much thought to see such stories as reflections of God's will expressed through love rather than law. We too must find out what pleases the Lord, and then live in that pleasure with freedom and joy. When we lay down our rules and live by love, God's will expands and we can say as the psalmist does, "The boundary lines have fallen for me in pleasant places" (Psalm 16:6).

God's will does not require that I put to death my own will. Instead, living in God's will requires that I exercise self-will or self-determination by choosing to follow him. God never destroys free will, for it's his greatest gift, endowed to humanity alone, and the sole means whereby we practice and experience love. Without self-will we have no ability to love, for love is a commitment that requires a moment-by-moment choice. When Scripture speaks of "dying to self" and "losing your life" (Colossians 3:3; Luke 9:24-25), it infers dying to self-interest, self-seeking, self-importance, self-centeredness, self-promotion, self-gain. In the process of losing these *sins of the self,* we are invited to gain real life by choosing to engage our self-will with God's will.

This invitation to engage self-will in loving God is heard in Moses' charge to the Israelites on the brink of entering the Promised Land. He said, "I have set before you life and death, blessings and curses. Now choose life, so that you and your children may live and that you may love the LORD your God, listen to his voice, and hold fast to him. For the LORD is your life" (Deuteronomy 30:19-20). Always God holds out a choice to love and be loved. And choice denotes the point where self-will must be exercised.

THE WILL OF LOVE

If you haven't figured it out yet, this chapter is not intended to tell you specifically what God's will is or isn't for you. Only you and God can work that out. His will is vast. And that vastness multiplies exponentially as it refracts through individual lives to become a multifaceted prism of his love. While God's will is broad, it emanates from a single source captured within the simple word *love.* He asks that we learn first how to receive love and then how to share the love we've received with others.

Receive love. We're born to receive love. As children we thrive on love, we crave it, seek after it, or wither for lack of it. But as adults, we put on the grown-up, be-responsible, take-care-of-business façade and easily forget how to receive love with childlike expectation.

One morning a backyard neighbor, whom I had never met, came to my front door to let me know that he was going to be working in his yard and would trim my overgrown bougainvillea bushes that were hanging over our common wall into his property. He assured me that he was happy to do it and would try to make sure the branches would fall on his side so he could clean them up. This was an incredible act of kindness on his part and a gesture of love from God who knew that yard maintenance was one of the biggest challenges for me to manage.

But rather than receiving this as an expression of love, I immediately felt so guilty and embarrassed about the inconvenience I was causing that as soon as he left I began to cry! I had neglected my yard for so long that it had become more than I could handle. Now the kindness of this neighbor laid bare that feeling of inadequacy within me. I thought of ways I could repay him and his family for taking care of my overgrown bushes — maybe a gift card or a batch of cookies, not as a pure expression of gratitude but as a way to ease my guilt. That incident helped me realize what difficulty I have in freely receiving love, and I'm asking God to help me learn this lesson.

First of all, I'm putting aside the fairy-tale belief that I can do everything for myself without anyone's help. I simply don't know how to do everything, don't have the equipment or resources to accomplish it all, and often am overwhelmed by how to make it happen. God's will that I receive his love means I must at times seek help and allow others to love me enough to lend a helping hand. This is the condition of all humanity, and the reason why God asks us to live in community in this way, for neighbors to help neighbors and friends to help friends. For until I can receive God's love as an act of his will, I will never be able to fully give that love to others.

Receiving love begins with acknowledging this need for love, support, and a helping hand. And in acknowledging that need, I become a child again as I learn to unapologetically seek after love, ask for it, and thrive in it. "Unless you change and become like little children, you will never enter the kingdom of heaven. Therefore, whoever humbles himself like this child is the greatest in the kingdom of heaven" (Matthew 18:3-4). Children are completely dependent on the love and generosity of others to survive because they have nothing of their own to offer. This is the reason a child is also the most open and willing to receive love.

Give love. How we express God's will to love others varies from person to person. We are not given a checklist of dos and don'ts, shoulds and shouldn'ts. We are not products of cookie-cutter theology that makes us all act and react in the same way. We must learn to trust God's ability to love us and to love others through us in the most unique ways. But if you really insist on a checklist to determine whether you are loving others, Paul came up with a good one, recorded in 1 Corinthians 13:4-7. In a nutshell it says: Love is patient, kind, protecting, trusting, hopeful, persevering, and rejoicing in truth. Love is not envious, boastful, proud, rude, self-seeking, easily angered, a scorekeeper of wrongs, or delighting in evil.

This list helps us recognize and develop love as we learn to share it with others. But as idealistic as "loving the world" may sound, love often comes down to difficult choices that demand great depth of character. It's more than dipping soup at the rescue mission or singing Christmas carols every year at the nursing home. It's easy to love when everyone is happy and we're feeling good about being nice to strangers, or living on the honeymoon of romance.

The virtues seen in a heart of love come to light when we're tested by irritating habits of others and we need to offer patience. It's when we must set aside our preferred way of doing things and compromise, or when we adjust our schedules to accommodate someone else. It's choosing to wave and smile rather than honk and gesture. It's sticking together because of that vow to abide "for better or worse." It means having an honest conversation to confront the destructive behavior of a family member. Love really listens and responds to the old man across the street who talks endlessly about nothing in particular. And it's offering forgiveness when the wound is still raw. There's nothing easy about giving love, but there is also nothing so delightful as joining my will to God's will. He promises that in loving each other we come to know him and love him. And in loving each other we become whole.

One of my favorite stories about the will of God comes from an interview with the woman who epitomized giving and receiving love. An American reporter asked Mother Teresa, "How do you know that this is truly God's will for you, that you're doing the will of God in this place of poverty, sickness, and hunger?" She smiled and explained, "That question is such an American ideal. I do not *do* the will of God. . . . I *am* the will of God."

Isn't it a relief to know that God's will is not a list of rules but rather a way of life?

God's will is vast because his love is endless. But at the same time, God's will is specific because his love is personal. The virtues of the heart teach us that it's not what we do but who we are and how we choose to love that help us end the battle of the will and simply rest in love.

BREAK THROUGH

1. To what extent have you discerned God's will in your life? What word would you use to describe God's will: a *mystery*, a *motivator*, an *answer*, a *frustration*, or some other word? How has your understanding of God's will changed over time?

2. When have you felt at odds with God's will? How were you able to resolve it? Spend time this week reading over the four short chapters in the book of Jonah in the Old Testament.

What do you learn about God's will through this reading? How do you relate to Jonah? What do you think God would have you know about your own life through this message?

3. What does God's will look or feel like in your life right now? Search for a symbolic reminder of the freedom found in God's will. Be creative. It may be the act of planting a garden, or painting a picture. It may be a word written on a smooth stone, or a hike through a park, a forest, or up a mountainside. Whatever you choose, offer it as a prayer, asking God to use it to reveal his leading in your life.

4. Revisit the Scriptures and quotation at the beginning of this chapter. How do Merton's words speak to you about God's will?

TEN

BREAK THROUGH TO WHOLENESS

And they devoted themselves to the apostles' teaching and the fellow-ship, to the breaking of bread and the prayers. And awe came upon every soul, and many wonders and signs were being done through the apostles. And all who believed were together and had all things in common. . . . And day by day, attending the temple together and breaking bread in their homes, they received their food with glad and generous hearts, praising God and having favor with all the people.

ACTS 2:42-47, (ESV)

Is not the cup of thanksgiving . . . a participation in the blood of Christ? And is not the bread that we break a participation in the body of Christ? Because there is one loaf, we, who are many, are one body, for we all partake of the one loaf.

1 CORINTHIANS 10:16-17

Christianity is not a purely intellectual, internal faith. It can only be lived in community. Perhaps for this reason, I have never entirely given up on church. At a deep level I sense that church contains

*something I desperately need. Whenever I abandon church for
a time, I find that I am the one who suffers. My faith fades, and
the crusty shell of lovelessness grows over me again. I grow colder
rather than hotter. And so my journeys away from church have
always circled back inside.*

PHILIP YANCEY[1]

One early Sunday morning, as I sipped coffee in my pj's, the deep
question of the divine mystery came to me in words from the eighties band The Clash, "Should I stay or should I go?" Stay home or go
to church, that is. Considering that I have "belonged" to a church
most of my life and have loved every church where I've attended
(I mean really loved the church, not just the experience, but the
church), I was puzzled by the mere idea that I would consider *not*
going to church on this Sunday morning, so I began to explore why
I was suddenly reluctant.

Over the past decade I had attended a small community church
that became like home to me and my family. We all shared life events
together: births and deaths, victories and setbacks, gains and losses.
We had built a spiritual history together throughout the years.
When my marriage fell apart, the congregation rallied round, offering words of comfort and prayers of support. But there was more.
Family after family provided for my very real physical needs. One
couple, knowing my need for reliable transportation, came to my
door one day with car keys and the title to one of their cars signed
over to me! Another family gave me furniture, and a group of young
men moved my entire household into our new, smaller home. This
stream of God's provision bound our hearts even closer together.

That's why it was so hard, when the church was hit with unexpected financial burdens, to close the doors on our place of worship and move into other congregations and the larger body of Christ. Now, two years later, I was still going through the motions of feeling at home in my new church. For the first time in all my "religious" experiences I felt disconnected, lonely, and discouraged, wondering if I'd ever find true fellowship and a growing faith again. For the first time I wondered, *Should I stay or should I go?*

In the midst of families, even generations of families, and couples who sit shoulder to shoulder in the service, I arrive without spouse or friend or family. I try to get to know the people sitting near me, asking God to help me make the "passing of the peace" a true gift of giving and receiving hospitality in the name of Christ. Of course I'm not the only "single," but the loneliness inside becomes inflamed in this setting. This is an odd realization, considering that the church is a community defined by love and connection and fellowship.

Yet this struggle to fit in and find my place gives me a good idea of what it feels like for others who are seeking God for the first time through a faith community. I'm choosing to believe that this struggle is part of God's purpose in this season of my life, trusting that he is already working out a plan and using it to strengthen me and his church. This thought alone begins to ease the heartache.

MORE THAN ME

I go to church for one simple reason: Because God calls us to *be* the church, the literal body of Christ, the embodiment and dwelling place of his presence. It seems to me one of the greatest callings, the highest purpose for anyone who calls herself a Christ-follower. Despite how often we may hop from church to church in search of the place that fits who we are, where we feel at home, there is a divine mystery that does not allow the church to be defined by the whim of our current felt needs or personal dilemmas. The church is God's doing. "*God* arranges the body . . . *God* combines the members . . . *God* appointed in the church gifts of healing and helping" (1 Corinthians 12:18,24,28, paraphrased). So I go. I squirm inside my skin over the temporary discomfort of my struggle, but I go because I am the church.

While I may emotionally feel alone, I am not. Just as a single hand, unique in its ability and purposes, is part of the whole body, so I am part of a greater whole, the body of Christ. In this place I am comforted to know, whether I see it or not, that I am participating in God's greater purpose. This is my call, my privilege, and my challenge all in one.

Recently, the pastor read those words from Acts 2 that describe the attributes of the first church in Jerusalem. He pointed out key words — "*Devoted . . . filled with awe . . . everything in common . . .*" — and challenged the congregation to rethink what it means to be the church. I reflected on those words and sensed how far my attitude had taken me away from that reality. My list of key words included: "*uncommitted . . . filled with questions . . . nothing in common.*" In order to understand how I could move from my reality to the biblical ideal, I began meditating on the following attributes from Acts 2:42-44 as a means of connecting more deeply with the community of believers and committing more fully to its spiritual vitality.

Devoted. This old-fashioned word conjures up a loving and faithful commitment to someone or something. Can I be devoted when I'm new to a congregation and feel like an outsider? Yes, I can be devoted to finding my place, and devoted to developing an internal attitude of compassion toward these people I don't yet know. I can be devoted to simply come, to contribute, if only by my physical presence.

The New Testament calls us to be devoted in several ways. Acts 2:42 says "They devoted themselves to the apostles' teaching and to the fellowship." If I'm devoted to the teaching, then I'm listening as if God himself were talking to me, which of course he is. And perhaps the writer of Acts connected teaching with fellowship because unless we process the teaching with others, it's difficult to truly learn.

When the teaching on Sunday morning encourages me to take an action, or let go of something, or reconsider a thought or attitude, I receive it as my God-given assignment for the week and use it as a tool to draw near to God by drawing near to others in some way. I turn the teaching into an opportunity for fellowship. For example, sometimes I'll send a simple note to the pastor or worship leader, letting that person know how God is using the message in my daily life. Or the teaching may nudge me to change in the way I interact with someone at work. When I find a way to make real-life human connections from the teaching of God's Word, I am allowing the "word of Christ to dwell in [me] richly" (Colossians 3:16) and at the same time creating fellowship through such connection.

We are also called to devote ourselves "to prayer, being watchful and thankful" (Colossians 4:2). I like this triune connection of praying with watching and gratitude. This puts me in a posture of holy expectation. I know when I devote myself to pray for my church, its leaders, its members, its activities, I'm asking and expecting God to show up and make a difference. I'm watching for that difference within me, or those with whom I interact, and I'm looking for reasons to give God thanks and praise. Each time I turn to God with my faith community on my mind, he seems to bind my heart a little closer to theirs.

Filled with awe. Actually the Scripture in Acts 2:43 states: "Awe came upon every soul" (ESV). This is different from the popular idea that we can be led into a sense of awe through an emotion evoked through a song or a story. Not that God doesn't use these acts of worship to make us aware of his presence and his splendor, but I get a sense that the awe that came upon every soul in the church in Acts was something more.

I can't say that this happens in most churches on any given Sunday. Some days I "feel" worshipful, other days I don't. But the closest I've come to experiencing this sense of "awe come upon every soul" was in a church that routinely called the congregation to moments of silence just before receiving the teaching of the morning. Not silence with background "mood" music — just plain silence.

For those few moments it seemed that standing silent before God stripped away self-conscious thoughts and pretense from the entire congregation. We set aside any "show" of church and became the church submitting our lives to the scrutiny of the Spirit, inviting him to search us and know our hearts (see Psalm 139:23). Each individual made room in the silence to turn toward God with a burden, a joy, a distraction, a sin. Together we took a collective deep breath and became conscious of the holy in a communal posture of openness and expectancy, as vessels longing to be filled by the power that makes us one.

Everything in common. I've come to believe that there is really only one thing we truly have in common, and that is the holy ground found at the foot of the cross of Christ. It is central to everything . . . the literal "crux" of the matter. The cross is why we come to church, it's where we are changed, it's how we are saved, it's what we cling to, and it defines who we are. Regardless of how "uncommon" I may feel among these people who are still strangers to me, this *one* thing, the cross, is *everything.* And I can truly say we share *everything* in common. On those Sunday mornings when I am aware of this, I don't feel so alone. I feel grateful to be part of a larger good.

This is never more evident than when we come to the communion table where Jesus' words take on new meaning. When I hear his words, "This is my body given for you" (Luke 22:19), I believe he is talking about all of us as the body of Christ. He is looking at all of us as one, as his broken body given to each other to share. Together our lives become a prayer: *We are your body, broken and offered back to you and to each other.* And while we individually are broken, we are never broken apart from one another. We are broken yet bound together as one body with bandages of swaddling clothes and a torn garment fallen from the cross and divided among us.

The Savior comes to the world to bind us together. His death anoints us with the salve of peace. His wounds wash, bandage, and heal us. Our brokenness is labeled loneliness, addiction, hatred, discontentment, dishonesty, and a host of other soul maladies. But our brokenness is not a fatal injury. Our dis-eased lives are not terminal afflictions. We will be cured. We are being cured. We are cured through Jesus' broken body as we become the broken body, the church.

UNEARTHING GOD'S COMMUNITY

I realized recently that nearly all of Jesus' life was lived in community (with the exception of time alone to pray and the time when he was tempted in the wilderness). He taught, healed, revealed, ate, worked, and traveled in the company of others, typically at least two others if not a multitude. And after his resurrection he continued to appear to groups of people. In the one instance where he spoke to Mary alone at the tomb, he instructed her to return to the others as well.

Each time Jesus showed up, the group experienced breakthrough. The two disciples on the road to Emmaus, confused and disheartened about Christ's death, broke through to enlightenment, their hearts burning within them, when they saw Jesus bless and break the bread around the table in their own home (see Luke 24:13-35).

Thomas was absent from the group when Jesus first appeared to the apostles. But when they bore witness of the living Christ, Thomas longed for his own experience with Jesus, to see with his eyes and touch him with his own hands. In community, Jesus honored Thomas's desire and appeared again, leading Thomas to break through from doubt to faith as he proclaimed, "My Lord and my God!" (John 20:28).

But my favorite post-resurrection story occurs with the downhearted apostles in their fishing boat. They seemed to have come nearly full circle as they cast their net on the water only to haul it in empty. In this frustration perhaps John was remembering their first encounter with Jesus when they were having equal success at catching fish. Then someone from shore calls to them, "Friends, haven't you any fish? . . . Throw your net on the right side of the boat and you will find some" (John 21:5-6). I can almost see a smile spread across John's face as he looks up, shields his eyes to see more clearly, and says without question, "It is the Lord!" With that, Peter jumps into the water and swims and splashes his way with passion toward Jesus, who is tending the hot coals. The scent and sizzle of grilling fish assures him that his Master is alive and well, sharing, partnering, ready to restore Peter and unearth his faith once again.

I know how Peter feels. It's easy for me to miss Jesus, to miss God at work in my world, unless I'm with others who are scanning the shoreline looking for Christ, expecting him to show up and are willing to point me in his direction, especially when I'm discouraged or lonely. That's when I realize that the completion of my faith happens when I'm present with other faithful believers. I'm not willing to settle for a partial awareness of God, or to occasionally nod my head in his direction. I'm not willing to toss church aside and forfeit the wholeness of my faith experience simply because I'm a little discouraged. I'm not willing to miss out on touching Jesus when others bear witness of his reality.

Should I stay or should I go? Today I am compelled to go, praying, watching, and expecting God to be revealed in the weak and the strong, in our singing and in our silence. In these people the incarnate spirit of unity comes to life in the places where we work, the homes where we live, the church where we gather. We bring a mixed bag of life circumstances, the lonely and busy, the needy and happy, the desperate and compassionate. But we bring it all to Jesus and gather around the fire of burning coals where I find the passion of companionship within the fellowship of believers.

As I look at the faces of those around me, even those I have yet to meet, I know even now that I am deeply devoted to them. I reach for the bread and the cup, awestruck by this sense of being a vital part of Christ's body. And I see the aloneness so common among us fades away as we come together in Jesus' name. We stand on common ground . . . holy ground at the foot of the cross. Together we walk in the wholeness of resurrected faith, hope, and love.

BREAK THROUGH

1. Refer to the opening quote from Acts 2:42-47, which describes the life of the first church. Which of these attributes can you relate to your own church life? Which areas are a mystery or challenge to you? Which areas would you like to explore further?

2. In what ways have you experienced or witnessed aspects of loneliness in the faith community? How can the church respond to the loneliness or disconnection within the faith community? How can the church respond to loneliness within the community at large?

3. This week experiment with creating a regular time and place for silence both within your daily life but also in the time you enter into worship with your faith community. You may want to arrive early before the service begins and pray over the space, the seats, the lives that will be entering in. Within your small group, experiment with the idea of remaining silent in a prayer time together until one feels led by God's Spirit to open the dialogue.

4. What new ideas about the faith community have come to life in you through these thoughts and your experimentation? How might it change your church experience?

5. Return to the Scriptures and quotations at the beginning of the chapter. Consider the passage from 1 Corinthians 10:16. How is sharing in a faith community at the communion table an active "participation in the body of Christ?" Respond to these ideas in your journal.

FINDING THE REAL YOU

My youngest daughter, Amy, told me recently, "You've changed, Mommy." I asked her to explain.

"You're more relaxed — cooler."

I smiled. "Is that an okay change for you?"

"Yeah," she smiled back.

I have a feeling that my change has more to do with her maturing than with my "break through" into some higher degree of coolness. But I hear such high praise from my teen as God's way of saying, "You're relaxing and finding your true self." And I sense that he's smiling too. Yes. We've made progress, but there is still much more road to travel and new horizons to discover and explore.

I'm learning to look with raw honesty at who I am in light of who God is and I see new life and emotion return to me, like a forest regreens itself after a devastating fire, or as a rosebush blooms after its pruning, or as a seedling pushes toward light after entering the dark earth. I've learned along the way that a heart tendered by the hand of God is not a weak heart, but rather a sensitive heart, able to discern another's pain and to comfort a grieving soul. It is a strong heart able to move with confidence in the freedom of God's will.

It is a pure heart, finding my identity from the sole source of truth found in the love of God. And it is a hopeful heart, moving me on toward the greater goal to find the kingdom of God within me.

As I encounter hard circumstances that may lie ahead on this journey, I know I'll continue to unearth new treasure found in God's image, which is hidden in my inner being. I'll continue to be awed by the paradox of how God keeps my heart strong and gentle, free and submitted, truthful and graceful, resting and growing. His words, gleaned from the pages of this journey, now echo through my mind as I hear him say:

> *O my people . . . I will keep you and bless you and make my face shine upon you. . . . In all your distress, I too am distressed . . . yet I desire truth in the inner parts where the treasures of heaven await your discovery. . . . Let me show you the full extent of my love. . . . I am the compassionate and gracious God, slow to anger, abounding in love and faithfulness, maintaining love . . . filling you to the measure of all my fullness through the Living Word . . . Let that word dwell in you richly as we share the dialogue of words and silence . . . for my kingdom is within you. . . . Come near to listen, to join with others whose hearts I strengthen as I call out to you. . . . O my people.*

God welcomes you every moment of every day to simply be yourself. He runs to greet you and invites you to see the breathtaking vista where his perpetual faithfulness strengthens your inner being. He spreads out the grassy hillsides where his good grace gives rest and renews your mind. And even in the dark valleys the light of his fierce love breaks through with joy to transform your life and unearth the divine beauty of your true heart. And amazingly, that point of breakthrough is not the end of the road but rather the place where real adventure begins.

BREAK THROUGH SMALL GROUP INSIGHTS

Whether you just met Jesus last week or have walked with him for decades, every Christ-follower has a longing to grow up spiritually, to know God more deeply and to see, over time, that knowing him has made a difference. But it's easy to allow our spiritual growth to "coast along." We make efforts to attend church, maybe to occasionally read the Bible, but we don't give much thought to whether we're growing spiritually or not.

Making a commitment to a small group can help you become intentional in your growth in Christ. Through such a group we develop spiritual roots, increase our faith (which is our God-confidence), and instill a hunger and thirst for God that will lead us to lean on him, learn of him, and love him more each day.

I've rarely been without a small support group in my life. I'm not even sure how other people get along without such a group. So I offer these suggestions and words of encouragement to you who may not have such a group but would like to start a Break Through Group:

1. Make it your goal to help create an environment where the women within your group feel safe in working through those tough situations of life. The small group is a tool for God to demonstrate his tenderness to us. But some come to a new small group fearful of uncovering long-festering heart-wounds. Some may choose not to become vulnerable. Your

attitude will help instill confidence in others that the time set aside to be together is God's invitation to enter a place of sanctuary.

2. Before you arrive each week, ask God to make each woman, beginning with you, ready and open to receive his word and to speak in truth and grace. Ask him to prepare your minds for new understanding and insight into his personality.

3. When you come together for the first time, do not begin the study until you've discussed the following three essential elements to create a strong, meaningful small group experience:

    ❧ Confidentiality: While you should feel free to share general concepts, teachings, and new insights with others outside your group, it is critical that everyone in the group keeps in confidence everyone's personal sharing. This is the emotional safety net you hold out to each other as you fall into the safe place of God's arms. The more honest and open your group (and you may need to lead the way by sharing your own heart first), the more open others will be to receive God's healing.

    ❧ Commitment: Commit to meet in the same place and time each week, or as frequently as you agree works for your group. Commit to faithful attendance. This solidifies the group and creates trust even beyond your meeting time. Women will know they can depend on each other. Commit to pray for one another at least once during the week. Make every effort to prepare and study ahead of time if appropriate. The best discussions are based on the discovery process that occurs through study during the week.

❦ Covenant: Either in writing or verbally, covenant with one another to honor the agreement to confidentiality and commitment in an effort to come to a place where hearts are transformed. A simple group covenant may read something like the one shown below. You can edit or add, or make these thoughts fit your own group dynamic. Don't get too specific here by adding in details about bringing refreshments or providing babysitting. Those are the business details of how a group operates. This group covenant is the heart of how the group connects:

Small Group Covenant

Coming together as a small group, we are a reflection of the Body of Christ. As such, we covenant together to . . .

❦ Encourage one another in our daily lives.

❦ Respect the confidentiality with which we share our lives by keeping our expressed words and thoughts within the confines of our meeting place.

❦ Commit to regular attendance to encourage one another in our meeting.

❦ Keep Christ as the center of all our conversations and to recognize his presence in each life represented.

Together, may your time in God's Word and in fellowship with his Spirit and with each other renew your souls and bind your hearts in his unity of love.

Notes

CHAPTER TWO

1. John Muir, "Three Adventures in the Yosemite," *Century* magazine, March 1912, quoted in *The Weathering Grace of God* by Ken Gire (Ann Arbor, MI: Servant Publications), 21.

CHAPTER THREE

1. Kathleen Norris, *Dakota: A Spiritual Geography* (New York, NY: Houghton Mifflin, 1993), 25.
2. Sir Alfred Tennyson, quoted in *Treasury of Familiar Quotations* (New York, NY: Avenel Books, 1963), 129.

CHAPTER FOUR

1. Tricia McCary Rhodes, *Taking Up Your Cross* (Minneapolis, MN: Bethany House, 2000), 11.
2. Amy Carmichael, compiled by Judith Couchman, *A Very Present Help* (Ann Arbor, MI: Servant Publications, 1996), 65.
3. Thomas Pierson, quoted in C. H. Spurgeon, *The Treasury of David* (MacLean, VA: MacDonald Publishing, n.d.), 2:8.

CHAPTER FIVE

1. Teresa of Avila, "The Interior Castle," in *Majestic Is Your Name*, ed. David Hazard (Minneapolis, MN: Bethany House, 1993), 36.

2.   Craig Childs, *The Secret Knowledge of Water* (Seattle,WA: Sasquatch, 2000), 267.

3.   Hannah Whitall Smith, quoted in *A Gentle Spirit Journal* (Uhrichsville, OH: Barbour, 2000).

CHAPTER SIX

1.   Julian of Norwich, quoted in *Praying with Julian of Norwich*, by Gloria Durka (Winona, MN: Saint Mary's Press, 1989), 42.

CHAPTER SEVEN

1.   Robert Benson, *Living Prayer* (New York, NY: Jeremy P. Tarcher/Putnam, 1998), 112-113.

2.   Henri Nouwen, *Spiritual Direction: Wisdom for the Long Walk of Faith* (New York, NY: HarperSan Francisco, 2006), 87. Nouwen adds a fourth path of "speaking the word through silence," which is discussed in chapter 8.

3.   Nouwen, 91.

4.   Quoted by Roger Housden in *How Rembrandt Reveals Your Beautiful, Imperfect Self: Life Lessons from the Master* (New York, NY: Harmony Books, 2005), 27.

5.   Mrs. Charles E. Cowman, *Streams in the Desert, vol. 2* (Grand Rapids, MI: Zondervan, 1966).

CHAPTER EIGHT

1.   Francis of Assisi, quoted in *Christian Spirit*, ed. Judith Fitzgerald and Michael Oren Fitzgerald (Bloomington, IN: World Wisdom, 2004), 146.

2.   Karen Mains, *The God Hunt: The Delightful Chase and Wonder of Being Found*, (Downers Grove, IL: InterVarsity, 2003).

CHAPTER NINE

1.   Thomas Merton, *New Seeds of Contemplation* (New York, NY: New Directions, 1961), 14.

CHAPTER TEN

1. Philip Yancey, *Church: Why Bother?* (Grand Rapids, MI: Zondervan, 1998), 23.

AUTHOR

MARSHA CROCKETT is an award-winning author who writes and speaks with a heart touched by God. Her mission in life is to unveil God's presence in the ordinary corners of life. She has authored four books and contributed to six others, including the *Couple's Devotional Bible*. She speaks to women's groups, in churches, at writer's conferences, and retreat settings. She also leads workshops in the business world on stress reduction, career building, and defining success.

Her Writer's Retreats, *Beyond Words*, inspire attendees to explore the divine possibilities of life through writing, journaling, and language as an open door to the "inner place" where God speaks to each of us.

Marsha lives in Phoenix, Arizona, with her two daughters. She is involved in her local church, seeking ways to help others find their niche and hone their God-given gifts.

Contact Marsha through her website at www.marshacrockett .com